MW01029023

The Final Missing Piece of
Ben Hogan's
Secret Puzzle

GRIP

WAGGLE

PRONATION

The *Final*
Missing Piece of
Ben Hogan's
Secret Puzzle

CUPPED
LEFT
WRIST

ARM
SPACING

DOWNSWING PLANE

HIP TURN

?

BALL POSITION

V.J. Trolio
with Dave Hamilton

Drawings by
Brent Raklovits

SUPINATION

The Final Missing Piece of
Ben Hogan's
Secret Puzzle

V. J. Trolio
with
Dave Hamilton

VJE, LLC

The Final Missing Piece of Ben Hogan's Secret Puzzle

V. J. Trolio with Dave Hamilton

Drawings by Brent Raklovits

VJE, LLC
Shannon, Mississippi

Copyright 2007 by V. J. Trolio with Dave Hamilton
All rights reserved.

Second Printing

VJE, LLC
P.O. Box 394
Shannon, Mississippi 38868

Edited by Tim O'Connor

Cover design and graphic artwork by
Dave Hamilton and Lindsey Christian

Trolio, V. J. with Hamilton, Dave. The Final Missing Piece of Ben Hogan's Secret Puzzle / V. J. Trolio with Dave Hamilton.

ISBN 978-0-9793635-0-4

Printed in the United States of America

To Allison and Maggie

Contents

The heirs of the Hogan Estate have requested that all of their royalties from this book be donated to the new nonprofit Ben Hogan Foundation. The mission statement for The Ben Hogan Foundation is below:

"The Ben Hogan Foundation is dedicated to honor, celebrate, and preserve the legacy and character of Ben Hogan through support of organizations that promote the game of golf and charities that reflect Mr. Hogan's core values."

Acknowledgments

The process of writing this book was much like the process of figuring out Hogan's secret: I could not have done it alone. I would like to thank all of those involved for their support and help, and most of all, our Lord.

Dave and I are grateful to our wives, Allison Trolio and Maggie Hamilton. It takes a unique woman to marry and live with a dedicated golfer, and these two women are the very best!

A very special thanks to Joey Hamilton for his applied science and math—again.

Thanks also to Tim O'Connor for his historical perspective and professional editing, to Lindsey Christian for her patience, efficiency and gifted artistry, and to Brent Raklovits for his excellent drawings.

A special thanks to the heirs of the Hogan Estate for their cooperation and very pleasant assistance. Also, thanks to Clem Darracott for his timely home movie of Ben Hogan and his contribution to the discovery of the *final missing piece* of Ben Hogan's secret puzzle, and to Tom McCarthy for access to his wonderful Ben Hogan Collection. These two men have helped keep the legend of Ben Hogan alive, and the pictures of Hogan in this book are the product of their work. Most of the pictures were digitized from 40-year-old eight-millimeter film. The contents of these never-before-printed action pictures of Ben Hogan far outweighs any lack of photographic quality.

I want to thank many of my players, especially four. (You know who you are.) Your desire and ability on the golf course and the friendships that have grown off the course led to most, if not all, of the constant questions that lingered in my mind. Once we stop asking questions, we stop finding answers.

Thanks to the following who have helped make this book a success: Mark Blackburn, Key Blair, Sandy Blair, Nancy Bruce, Dr. Greg Childrey, Cissye Gallagher, Jim Gallagher Jr., Dr. Brian Garman, Irene Hamilton, Peter Kessler, Cheryl Leb, JoLene Lee, Jesse McNeese, Gordon Miller, Old Waverly Golf Club, Payton Osborn, Reese Roberson, Lisa H. Scott, Mary Jo Tate, Kelly Tippet, Johnny Tritt, Mary Jane Vaughan, Bill Walters, and Tim Yelverton.

I would also like to thank all of the instructors I have been fortunate enough to work with. Thank you for sharing your ideas, concepts, and theories about the game of golf.

Finally, thanks to the following authors and publishers for their cooperation with us on this book:

John Andrisani, *The Hogan Way*, © 2000 by Harper Collins, New York, New York. Used by permission. All rights reserved.

Clem Darracott, *Ben Hogan: In Pursuit of Perfection*, DVD © 1995 by Clem Darracott Incorporated. Used by permission. All rights reserved.

James Dodson, *Ben Hogan: An American Life*, © 2004 by Doubleday. Used by permission. All rights reserved.

Bill Fields, "A Champion's Last Hurrah", © 2007. Originally published in *Golf World*. Reprinted by permission of the Hogan Estate. All rights reserved.

Ben Hogan, *Five Lessons: The Modern Fundamentals of Golf*, © 1957 by Simon & Schuster, New York, New York, 10020. Used by permission. All rights reserved.

Life magazine, April 5, 1954 and August 8, 1955, © 1954 and 1955 by Life Inc. Used by permission. All rights reserved.

Thomas E. McCarthy, *The Ben Hogan Collection*, © by McTee's Champions LLC. Used by permission. All rights reserved.

Cary Middlecoff, *The Golf Swing*, © 1974 by Simon & Schuster, Inc. Used by permission. All rights reserved.

Herbert Warren Wind, *The Story of American Golf*, © 1975 by Random House, Inc. Used by permission. All rights reserved.

Preface

This book is not titled *The Secret of the Golf Swing*, nor is it titled *The Easy Way to Learn Golf*. Instead it is an analysis of the swing which Ben Hogan actually used in competition, after his car wreck, and during the period when he was the dominant player in golf. If you have studied many of the fundamentals in *Five Lessons: The Modern Fundamentals of Golf* and you are willing to put in the time to master the drills in the back of this book, then you too can own a golf swing based on the model provided by Ben Hogan. All of the drills can be done at home. They are very simple, but a lot of repetitions are required to master each specific move.

This book is meant to explain Hogan's writings so that the average golfer can take *Five Lessons* and turn it into one of the most effective golf instructional books ever written. Almost all of *Five Lessons* is still relevant, with the exception of some sections that can be replaced with the information found in this book; these are noted in chapter 11.

The Final Missing Piece of Ben Hogan's Secret Puzzle fully supports Hogan's belief that the golf swing is dependent on the use of the body. Currently there are two schools of thought in golf about which plays a more prominent role in the swing: the hands and arms or the body—a kind of modern-day chicken-and-egg theory. It is my hope this book will begin to bring these two schools together so that we may better understand the relationship between the body, arms, and hands.

This book is not a method. It is an explanation of one man's method. Study and grow your own game with the help of a good instructor. The *missing piece*, which this book reveals, is special because the man regarded as the best ball-striker in the history of the game mastered it and then shrouded it in mystery.

Can it help your game? Absolutely! However, there is no one true secret to everyone's game; there are only geometry, math, and physics and the application of these sciences to your swing. If this book succeeds in answering some of your questions, makes striking a golf ball easier and more fun, and eliminates the left side of the golf course for you, then it will be a success. To make it easy for the majority of golfers, this book addresses right-handed players. It's our hope that left-handed golfers can easily adapt the technique to their swing.

The revelations about the golf swing in this book are as real as the earth beneath your feet. Implement them slowly, and you will improve if you understand the fundamentals that Hogan put forth in *Five Lessons*. Don't go too fast, and above all follow the drills and not your feelings alone. Beyond that, I hope you enjoy the dual journeys of golf and life. Hopefully, both will be long and pleasant.

Trolio

Chapter 1

History of the Secret and the Missing Piece

To most avid fans of Ben Hogan, the "secret" is an enduring mystery. Through the years, almost every Hogan book—whether instructional or biographical—has tried to determine the true nature of the secret.

The origins of the secret go back to Hogan's struggles early in his career. Since he turned professional at age 17 in 1930, Hogan had battled a random but nasty hook with his driver—the sniping kind that starts left, then ducks violently downward and into all kinds of trouble.

As a tournament player, he and his wife Valerie traveled the tour together. They lived very frugally, and he kept them afloat mainly through meager earnings from teaching lessons while winning very little cash in tournaments. For the better part of a decade, he fought both the hook and inconsistency. In 1938, with some financial backing and coaching from British professional Henry Picard, but mostly his own tenacity and hard work, Hogan won his first professional event—the Hershey Four-Ball Invitational with Vic Ghezzi.

The next year Hogan was getting very frustrated by the hooks that often showed up unexpectedly to destroy a round. Picard worked with Hogan at the 1939 PGA Championship and was quoted as saying, "Ben, in your case, it's pretty simple. You'll never win until you learn to slice the ball."[i] Picard moved Hogan's hands more to the left on the club, putting them in a more neutral position. Hogan quickly assimilated the lesson and drove the ball amazingly well, missing only three fairways in 36 holes. However, Paul Runyan putted lights out to beat him in the match play quarterfinals.

As somewhat of an introvert who generally disliked small talk and socializing with anyone he didn't know well or respect, Hogan appeared driven in his zeal to spend time alone practicing and figuring out the swing. While many professionals played cards between tournament rounds and whiled away the time in bars, Hogan worked tirelessly to improve.

In many ways Hogan is believed to have invented practice in golf.

He would work almost anywhere he could hit balls: practice areas at golf clubs, fields, schoolyards—any open space.

His work ethic began to pay off in the '40s when he started to win more consistently. Between 1940 and 1945, he won four to five events per year for a total of 20 victories. He was a solid player but had not yet risen to the rarified level of Sam Snead or Byron Nelson, both winners of major championships.

His problem was still the hook. "I had a low, ducking, agonizing hook, the kind you could hang your coat on," Hogan wrote in a famous *Life* magazine article in 1955. "When it caught the rough it was the terror of the field mice."[ii]

Thinking in bed in 1946 about his predicament apparently led to curing the hook and to his breakthrough season. That year, he remarkably won 13 times, including his first major, the PGA Championship. Sportswriters were fascinated by his devotion to practice, his apparent search for the perfect swing and the cocoon of concentration in which he immersed himself during tournaments.

That year, talk started to filter around that Hogan had developed some kind of secret move in his swing. The secret appeared to solve the left-of-left hook that had plagued his early career and kept him from golf's top rungs. As Hogan matured and became Snead's arch rival (Nelson had retired from competitive golf in 1946), he played few regular tour events and focused more on winning major championships.

He slyly played up the notion that he had a secret, and fans and reporters would occasionally ask him what it was. Hogan would not reveal it, which deepened the intrigue for some and made others more skeptical that there was a single mechanical move that had turned Hogan into a winner.

Snead was among the cynics. "Anybody can say he's got a secret if he won't tell what it is,"[iii] he said with derision. Asked for his opinion, Gene Sarazen just pointed to his head and said, "He has it up here."[iv]

Hogan won 7 times in 1947 and then captured 10 events in 1948 including 2 majors, the U.S. Open and the PGA Championship. He was the man in golf, but he also transcended the sport. His face graced the cover of *Time* magazine in January 1949.

Fig. 1 - Pre-1950 Hogan swing

Only a few weeks after the *Time* cover, Hogan played in the Phoenix Open, where he lost in a play-off to Jimmy Demaret. He and Valerie then loaded their car and headed home to Fort Worth.

They got as far as Van Horn, Texas, where they spent the night at the El Capitan Motel; the next morning they left on the final leg of their trip home. A Greyhound bus pulled into their lane to pass a truck on a foggy, icy, two-lane west Texas highway and collided head-on with Hogan's car. A split second before the crash, Hogan flung himself across Valerie in an effort to protect her. The courageous act probably prevented Hogan from being killed; the force of the collision rammed the steering wheel through the driver's seat.

Even so, Hogan suffered devastating injuries: a double fracture of the pelvis, a broken inner bone in his left ankle, a broken collarbone, and a fractured right rib. It appeared that he would never play in another championship.

It got worse. Sixteen days after the accident, blood clots began breaking loose from his injured legs and moving to his lungs, causing tremendous pain. Without the drugs and vena cava clamps or umbrellas available today, invasive surgery was the only way to guarantee that a larger clot would not break free, travel through his heart, and block the blood flow to his lungs. The main three-quarter-inch-diameter vein from his legs had to be quickly tied off at a point behind his internal organs and next to his spine.

The only doctor in the country who could perform this surgery was Tulane University medical professor Dr. Alton Oschner (who later founded the Oschner Clinic Foundation based in New Orleans). Through the efforts and connections of Hogan's brother Royal, the generosity of the United States Air Force, the prayers of Valerie Hogan, and the concern of a nation, Dr. Oschner was flown to El Paso on a B-29 bomber and performed the difficult and dangerous operation.

"The operation saved Hogan's life, but there was a stern possibility that he would be a lucky man indeed to be able to walk normally again, let alone resume the toil of tournament golf, where the invariable strain on a man's physique, his legs in particular, can be a terrible thing even for the hardiest of young men,"[v] Herbert Warren Wind wrote in *The Story of American Golf*.

After lying on his back for 58 days, Hogan finally recovered some mobility. And so began the comeback that seemed almost miraculous. "Hogan not only came back, . . .but . . . he demonstrated that he was a discernibly better golfer than he had ever been,"[vi] Wind wrote. Following the accident, Hogan's swing took on a different quality. Most observers—even fellow touring professionals and top instructors—could note a major difference in his performance compared to the late '40s. His swing had changed, but no one knew exactly how.

Hogan's bread-and-butter shot became a low penetrating fade, but he could also move the ball at will. His swing became a repeatable marvel of balance, elegance, and power. The speed of his swing in the hitting zone was incredible, his contact with the ball almost violent. The sound of impact was a loud crack that was uniquely his own.

After the accident his swing became machine-like, and he played fearlessly. He had good reason to feel confident: he had made his hook history. The adjustments gave him complete assurance that he would never again unintentionally hit the ball left. In fact, he took the left side of the golf course out of play. The Hawk had willed himself to ensure that the miserable left shot that had tormented him earlier in his career would never haunt him again.

Cary Middlecoff said that before the accident, Hogan was as inconsistent as most tournament professionals, scattering drives in the rough and imprecise with his irons. "It was in 1950 that he began showing the kind of precision golf that set him apart,"[vii] Middlecoff wrote in his book, *The Golf Swing.*

"In 1950, he began to take on the miracle-man aura. Small crowds that included a number of his fellow pros would gather around him and try to watch his every move anytime he started hitting practice balls,"[viii] said Middlecoff, the '55 Masters champ and winner of the '49 and '56 U.S. Opens.

Hogan focused almost solely on major championships, in part to save his strength for the events that were most important to him. His performance in these majors in the early '50s was a stretch of golf comparable to Harry Vardon's at the turn of the century, Bobby Jones' in the '30s, and Tiger Woods' in 2000. Seventeen months after the accident, Hogan won the 1950 U.S. Open—his second—at Merion, site of Hy Peskin's historic picture of his famous one-iron to the 18th green.

In 1951, he captured the Masters and his third U.S. Open. His only victory in 1952 was the Colonial Invitational, leading some to think that at 39, his best days were behind him, especially considering the toll the accident had taken on him.

Yet again, Hogan willed himself back and put together the greatest year of his career and one of the best in the history of the game. In 1953 he won the Masters, U.S. Open, and British Open, becoming the first golfer in history to achieve the feat. He certainly would have been a threat to win the PGA Championship—and thus the Grand Slam—but the event in Michigan conflicted with British Open qualifying. (At the time, most American pros did not usually play in the Open, citing the expense, often-bad weather, and unfamiliarity with links golf.) Upon his return to the United States from Scotland, he was feted with a ticker tape parade down Broadway in New York to commemorate his step into history.

In 1954, he lost the Masters to Snead by a stroke, and then he suffered another blow when he lost the 1955 U.S. Open at the Olympic Club to unknown Jack Fleck. Fleck birdied the last hole of regulation play to force a play-off the next day. Hogan came to the 18th tee of the play-off one stroke down. He needed a birdie, but his right foot slipped on sand atop the slightly top-dressed tee. His ball went left into deep rough, from which it took three shots to escape. Fleck made a par, while Hogan made a double bogey to lose the play-off by three strokes. Hogan's secret did not betray him, but one of its components did. Even with an extra spike in his right shoe, the slippery footing kept him from properly executing his swing. After that heartbreaking Open, Hogan announced he was going into semi retirement. Middlecoff edged him in the '56 Open, and the "Age of Hogan" was over.

The winner of nine major championships was an icon for his compelling story that was made into the 1951 movie *Follow the Sun*, for having conquered a tragedy (his father Chester committed suicide in front of him when he was nine), and for coming back from the horrific accident to become one of the all-time greats. Although he could be all smiles and provide good quotes after a victory, his distant and stern demeanor on the course made him mysterious.

As a golfer, Hogan had done what was considered impossible, even for the world's best players: he had mastered the golf swing. Just as golfers today are always looking for the Holy Grail of golf instruction that will show them the path to straighter and longer shots, golfers in the early '50s were entranced by the technical perfection of Hogan's elegant but powerful swing.

To take advantage of Hogan's retirement, his iconic celebrity status, and the continuing conjecture about his "secret," *Life* magazine ran a story in April 1954 in which he continued to taunt the golf world. He was quoted as saying, "I have a secret. . . . It is easy to see, if I tell you where to look."[ix]

In the article, five well-known professionals of the era postulated on what they thought the secret actually was. Snead said Hogan's hands never crossed over. Claude Harmon was close when he said his left hip leads: "Hogan's body doesn't turn, it just slides forward."[x] Fred Gronauer was even closer to identifying the *missing piece* when he stated "It's his pivot"; he then called Hogan's motion a "hula like pivot."[xi] Figure 2 below shows just how close he was, even though he missed by a bit with the left heel.

Fig. 2 - Fred Gronauer and his version of Ben Hogan's secret in 1954

The editors of *Life* had enticed the golf world with their 1954 article about Hogan's secret, and they convinced him with $10,000— which Hogan viewed as capital for his young equipment company— to follow it up with the famous 1955 story.

Under the headline "This Is My Secret," Hogan wrote that the mechanics of a good swing impart hook spin on the ball, mainly because the wrists roll over the top of the shaft just before impact. But, he wrote, "A hook is hard to judge. Maybe one week you will be able to judge it adequately, but then the next week you aim a little farther over to the right to compensate."[xii]

He said that he tried all the usual cures, such as opening his stance, changing his grip, and cutting across the ball. "They all worked but in the process, they cut down my distance by five to 10 yards. Five yards is a long way. . . . You can't correct a fault with a fault."

He disclosed that the secret consisted of two adjustments: first, he moved his left hand one-eighth to one-fourth inch to the left so the thumb was almost directly on top of the shaft. He described a second adjustment as "the real meat of the 'secret.'"

"I cupped the [left] wrist gradually backward and inward on the backswing so that the wrist formed a slight V at the top of the swing," he wrote. "This simple maneuver, in addition to the pronation, had the effect of opening the face of the club to the widest practical extreme at the top of the swing."[xiii]

Wind wrote that the net effect of these moves in combination locked "his left wrist so it could not roll over as he came into and through the ball."[xiv]

In the *Life* article, Hogan wrote, "At this point the swing had been made hook proof. . . . The result was that lovely, long-fading ball which is a highly effective weapon on any golf course."[xv]

And that was that. The secret had apparently been revealed.

However, not everyone was convinced that Hogan had disclosed his secret. Many tour players thought that Hogan had misled the magazine and purposefully held back on the true nature of the secret. Club professionals warned students that unless they were great players already, Hogan's secret was a recipe for slicing the ball.

The *Life* article set in motion events that led to the publication of his landmark book, *Five Lessons: The Modern Fundamentals of Golf.*

Over its 50-year life span, *Five Lessons* became the number-one-selling sports instruction book of all time. Combining Hogan's authoritative teaching and reputation as golf's ultimate ball-striker, Herbert Warren Wind's elegant phrasing, and the handsome pencil drawings of Anthony Ravielli, *Five Lessons* is still in high demand.

Most serious students of the golf swing own the book and have read it countless times. Thousands of golfers consider *Five Lessons* to be the definitive source on the fundamentals of the game.

Despite its high reputation, the book has confused and frustrated many of these same golfers. Applying Hogan's teachings has proven difficult for many readers.

Here's why: Hogan left out some very important information. While the book appears to contain all the pieces of the golf swing's complex puzzle, a key piece is missing.

It's our contention that Hogan deliberately withheld one key element of the secret. For five decades, the belief has persisted that SOMETHING WAS STILL MISSING and Hogan's secret was still just that—a secret.

Some instructors have argued that Hogan wrote about what he believed—moreover, what he felt—happened in his swing, but that he did not accurately describe what he actually did. To a certain extent, this is our belief also. In the area of swing planes, he wrote of his FEELINGS, which are very crucial to making a Hogan-like swing. Videos that Hogan never watched confirm that his club was NOT doing what he FELT and taught in *Five Lessons*. However, it is our contention that Hogan knew exactly what he was doing when it came to protecting his *missing piece*.

Like detectives, many Hogan history experts and some of golf's most esteemed instructors have tried to unravel the mystery. John Andrisani's book, *The Hogan Way*, published in 2000, included several well-known instructors who discussed Hogan's hip movement at the start of his downswing. Two of these professionals also came very close to his true secret.

The book's most insightful paragraph tells the story of professional Mike Austin playing with Hogan during his first complete round of golf after his car accident. During the round, Hogan told Austin about a dream he had while lying in his hospital bed. He dreamed of a body motion that turned around his left foot and leg, a movement that he had seen in the swing of an old Scottish pro named Jay Broune. Austin's story ends by telling us that Hogan proved dreams could come true, and Hogan did not hit a hook the entire round. This dream was never mentioned in *Five Lessons*, but it may have been a very important moment in the evolution of the golf swing.

Hogan maintained that the concepts in the 1955 *Life* article were his secret, but he certainly left the door open for conjecture. He later entered into negotiations with *Golf Digest* for the revelation of his true secret, but negotiations broke down when the price for this information got into the six-figure range.

When Hogan died in 1997 at the age of 84, it was generally accepted that the true nature of the secret was forever gone with him.

But now, after more than 50 years, Hogan's secret has finally been discovered. It's our sincere conviction that we have identified the *final missing piece* of Ben Hogan's secret puzzle.

We are excited to present it to you in hopes that it will help your golf game and significantly add to the body of knowledge about one of golf's magnificent obsessions—Ben Hogan's swing.

Chapter 2

What the Missing Piece Did for Ben Hogan. . . And What It Can Do for You

When Hogan fit the *missing piece* into his own puzzle—probably as he lay in the hospital in 1949—he accomplished three primary things:

1. He found a way to swing a golf club that eliminated the pull, the pull-hook, and left side of the golf course.

2. He created a golf swing capable of maximum efficiency and power because he used Newton's Second Law of Physics to its full effect. This enabled a short, small man to hit a wound, balata-covered golf ball 300 yards with a wooden driver.

3. He created a body motion that completely fit his arm swing. The sequence of Hogan's lateral motion and turn fit the connection of his arms to his body in the downswing-forward swing.

By adding the *missing piece* to your own golf game, you also can achieve these three admirable goals.

Most of us cannot emulate Tiger Woods, who possesses tremendous athleticism, a Herculean devotion to fitness, and almost unworldly control and power. However, the majority of golfers can relate to a golfer about five feet seven inches tall with an average build, severely damaged legs, and constant aches and pains.

Regardless of our body type, we can achieve great things through a constant search for knowledge, a strong work ethic, and a "never quit" attitude—three attributes which both Hogan and Woods have exemplified.

One of the first steps in your own journey to becoming a superior ball-striker is to master the fundamentals of the swing, including grip, posture, stance, and alignment. We suggest you start with Hogan's *Five Lessons*.

When you fill in the *missing piece* in combination with the solid fundamentals of Hogan, you can also eliminate the left side of the golf course, increase your body's rotational speed, learn to control your ball flight, and become a great shot-maker.

To begin any journey of self-improvement, we must become

aware of those things we need to change. Nearly all amateurs swing the club on an incorrect path, from outside to inside the target line. (The target line is a straight line drawn from the target through the ball and extending well behind you.) This outside-in move is also known as swinging "over the top." This occurs because most golfers shift onto their right leg on their backswing, and then try to turn their hips counterclockwise to start their downswing.

The result is usually the dreaded slice that haunts the majority of golfers or a pull that sends the ball well left of the target. With the erratic timing of most golfers plagued by an outside-in swing, they will hit some shots that slice way right and some that go dead left. Standing over the ball, they are not sure which shot will show up. That's called a two-way miss, and it's a very frustrating way to play golf.

In contrast, the swing of professionals and low-handicap players approaches the ball from inside the target line, which is why they fight pushes, hooks, and "getting stuck" (when the hips outrace the hands and arms).

To save the ball from starting right, many better players swing left through impact. However, most of these players have too much lateral motion onto their back leg during their backswing, and this does not allow an arm swing that resembles Hogan's. So, after a few "double-crossed" tee shots (where the ball starts left, then hooks) or toe strikes on the clubface, they return to their inside-out arm swing and learn to live with it.

This brings us back to Hogan. He learned to play a fade, which moves from left to right but has far less spin than a poor player's slice. (Remember Picard said Hogan had to learn to slice the ball?) And he attacked the ball from inside the target line without fear of going left.

Regardless of your current playing ability, Hogan's *missing piece* will help you. Your left shoulder will be farther forward at impact than it was at address, and your body will rotate faster. Now you will be able to hit the ball hard, releasing the hands and mirroring the images you see on page 102 of *Five Lessons*. It will also enable higher-handicap amateurs to attack the inside of the ball, possibly for the first time, and enjoy the power and precision they have long been seeking.

Finally, it will eliminate the pull, pull-hook, and the left side of the golf course. This will enable better players to swing as far left after impact as they wish. It will also provide them with additional power, increased precision, and the confidence to hit aggressive shots that lead to better scoring.

Hogan had to be elated when he perfected his "secret." You can now realize this joy as well.

©2007 BenHoganCollection.com

Fig. 3 - Ben Hogan at the "top"

Chapter 3

The Discovery of Hogan's Missing Piece

As a teaching professional, I am a golfer first and a teacher second. Even though I make my living teaching people how to play golf, I'm really like every other golfer: I love to play the game, experience different golf courses, and test my skills in competition. This is why, despite the odds against a teaching pro, I found myself in the hunt to qualify for the U.S. Open in 2005. I had shot 67 in the first round of the 36-hole final stage of Open qualifying. I was 18 holes away from playing in a major championship at Bethpage Black.

On the 11th hole during the second round at East Lake Golf Club in Atlanta, Georgia, I began to get my old "handsy feeling" back. I hated this feeling. I associated it with inconsistency and lack of control. I also knew that when I was under the gun, it caused me to pull-hook the ball and get into all kinds of trouble.

It was the same feeling that I had experienced throughout my career. By the 13th hole, I was four over par when torrential rain drenched East Lake and play was halted. Sitting at even par for the tournament, I had no chance of getting in the Open.

It was very discouraging. Despite all the practice and everything I knew as a teaching professional, when the pressure was on I was again sabotaged by the same handsy feeling. Disgusted, I packed up and came home.

This was the story of my playing career. Like that 67 in the first round of U.S. Open qualifying, I could really light up a golf course from time to time. I had modest success as a collegiate player at the University of Southern Mississippi, making it to the NCAA Regionals as an individual in 1997; and I did all right on the minitours for a few years. One of the turning points of my career was playing in the PGA Tour's Southern Farm Bureau Classic in Jackson, Mississippi, in 1999. From that experience I learned that there was a big difference between my swing and the dependable, repeatable golf swing of even the average touring pro.

I further learned that my shooting scores like 67 was dependent on making a bunch of putts and scrambling very well. The more I studied the best golfers, the more I understood that my ball-striking was below the level required to compete as a touring professional. All my life I just got the ball in the hole, relying more on my short game rather than proper mechanics.

I also eventually realized that I was better at teaching people how to play golf than I was at trying to make money playing golf. In fact, I was a very good golf instructor, and I quickly progressed through the ranks, working with and having success with beginners, juniors, amateurs, and tour players. Working at a great old club with golfers of all ability levels is a dream job.

But I still love to stay sharp and compete, and I have enjoyed wins in section events and top finishes in PGA national events. However, the bad old handsy feeling never went away, and I couldn't seem to stop it.

In working with tour professionals, top amateurs, and some great college players, I began to notice a common technique: these very good players stayed "on top of the ball." That is, the head moved very little during the swing, at impact the left wrist was flat as they struck the ball, and the clubhead and left arm formed a straight line as they swung under the forward shoulder. I have spent many hours teaching players to get into these perfect alignments.

Many of my teacher friends were very helpful in my research about the pivot (the movement of the body during the golf swing) and its relationship to the footwork and the arm swing. I am especially grateful to Mark Blackburn, teaching professional at Gunter's Landing in Guntersville, Alabama. Mark was there to share the moment when I made the discovery about Hogan's *missing piece.* As I researched and learned more about what Hogan was actually doing, Mark became a sounding board for many ideas and thoughts.

For my understanding of footwork, I owe a lot to my father Victor. In boxing, as in golf, much attention is paid to footwork and body movement. When I was growing up, my father pushed my brother William and me to box. When you are short and Italian growing up in the South, it is not a bad idea. In boxing you learn a lot about where your body is in space, especially your body's center of gravity. If you don't move correctly in the ring, the lightest of punches can knock you off balance, and you will be unable to throw a punch with any zing in it.

Through boxing I was able to appreciate Hogan's elegant footwork and especially his powerful body motion from the top, which made his swing seem effortless, athletic, and simple. Thanks, Dad, for throwing me into the ring.

The arm movement in the golf swing is another important motion, and in Hogan's case a unique one. In working with Payton Osborn, a great player and good friend, I noticed that Payton's arm action was very much like Hogan's: he takes it back on a flat plane, and the club moves quickly left after impact.

Payton's questions forced me to study the arm swing and its relationship with the pivot or body motion. I now understand that not every great player swings "left" after impact. Instead, good players have found an arm swing which matches their center of gravity motion during their swing. Hogan swung hard left, but almost all of his contemporaries—and many great modern-day players—did not. However, they all found an arm swing that perfectly matched the movement of their bodies. Thanks, Payton, for pushing me as an instructor and forcing me to understand this basic principle.

Further research into Hogan's swing reminded me of the concept of a tripod center, a *Golfing Machine* instruction term that describes the relationship between a player's feet and head. With a tripod center, the head remains steady through the motion of swinging the club.

This led me to a "centroid," a mathematical term, which is defined as "the center of mass of an object having constant density."[xvi] When I applied the idea of a centroid and a tripod center to Hogan's swing, I drew a line on a picture of Hogan at address that went straight down from his head. The line connected with his navel. His center of gravity was on that line.

In the human body, our center of gravity—also called the center of mass—is found roughly an inch and a half below the navel. However, for most adults, the human body is not of uniform density; it weighs more on the back half than the front half. The bone structure in the human body moves the center of mass inward toward the back of the body away from the navel. This means that the center of mass is somewhere between the navel and the spine, but closer to the spine. This center of gravity shifts with each body movement. However, the shifting of the center of gravity and the shifting of weight are one and the same. The difference between Hogan's swing and almost all others was the sequence or timing of his center of gravity's movement. A careful analysis of this fact led to the discovery of the *missing piece*.

I next looked at low point. The low point of the golf swing is located opposite the forward shoulder. This means the club reaches its lowest point opposite the left shoulder at impact. Also, the club reaches the most outward point (the toe of the club is farthest from the feet) when it is opposite the left shoulder. This creates a geometrical alignment that is fixed in every player. That's why it's crucial that golfers concentrate on proper ball positioning, pivot motion, and the correct use of the hands. When these are correct and move in sequence, the player can go to sleep on the way down and still strike the ball well.

This connection between center of gravity and the low point and the outward point of the swing became clear when I looked more closely at Hogan's swing, and it blew apart my convictions about the golf swing.

I noticed that when Hogan completed his backswing, he was in a fully coiled position with the majority of his weight over his foot— not his RIGHT foot, but his LEFT. His right leg was also angled toward the target much more than at address. All of the above is obvious when we do what Hogan challenged us to do: look in the correct place, which in this case is a rearview sequence of the man in competition.

This goes against conventional wisdom in golf. It's an accepted fundamental that you start with your weight about 50/50 on each foot at address. Then, as you pivot your upper body in the backswing, the majority of weight goes to the right foot. That is how I was taught to swing a golf club, and it is probably how you were taught.

When the majority of the weight moves over the LEFT foot on the backswing, many instructors consider it to be a "reverse pivot," but this is not correct. A true reverse pivot involves a forward lateral weight shift during the backswing and an opposite weight shift backward during the downswing. The term "reverse pivot" has taken on a negative connotation, and most golfers who consider themselves students of the swing consciously avoid this move.

Hogan most definitely did not have a reverse pivot. In fact, the post-accident Hogan moved his center of gravity forward in a sequence that enabled him to utilize Newton's Second Law of Motion. It also created perfect left arm-clubshaft alignments, and he did not hit the ball left anymore. As he began his downswing, his axis of rotation was anchored over the inside of his left foot, and his weight never moved backward during the swing. I repeat: Ben Hogan did not have a reverse pivot.

My analysis and understanding of Ben Hogan's golf swing would never have been possible without the contributions of engineer and friend Joey Hamilton and his ability to take my observations and find the math and science which explained what I was seeing on the video monitor. As he did with the Putting Arc training device, he took a complex motion and broke it down into basic scientific components. His technical support gave me the confirmation and confidence to keep working on this project, and for this I will always be appreciative.

When I began to apply this motion of Ben Hogan's *missing piece* to my own teaching, the changes among my students were incredible. Players who broke planes stopped breaking them. Players who couldn't take divots started taking divots. Players picked up clubhead speed.

And remember that "handsy feeling" that plagued my own swing and how I'd hit it left under the gun? That's history. Thank you, Mr. Hogan.

These are the key elements that went into the research and discovery of Hogan's *final missing piece*. Without many great people and their views of the golf swing, geometry, physics, and the human body, it would not have happened. I hope you enjoy the ride as much as I have.

Fig. 4 - Ben Hogan using the *missing piece*

Fig. 5 - A modern swing using the *missing piece*

Chapter 4

The Puzzle Pieces Hogan Gave Us in *Life* Magazine and in *Five Lessons*

Nearly all golfers who are serious about improvement will agree that the golf swing is indeed a puzzle. We are constantly searching for the correct pieces and trying to integrate them into a proper sequence of motion that produces quality golf shots. Hogan created a puzzle when he put his swing theories on paper in *Life* and in *Five Lessons*. The puzzle pieces he gave us have been key elements in the quest for improvement among modern golfers for more than five decades. This longevity in itself attests to the quality of his teachings.

The puzzle pieces from *Life* magazine are:
• Neutral left hand
• Wrist pronation on the backswing
• Cupped left wrist for a fade
• Flat left wrist for a draw

The major puzzle pieces from *Five Lessons* are:
• Grip
• Footwork
• Address alignment
• Arm motion
• Ball position
• Waggle
• Backswing sequence
• Downswing sequence
• Impact alignments
• Right arm action
• Swing plane

Since Hogan's "This Is My Secret" article in *Life* in 1955 and the publication of *Five Lessons* in 1957, many students of the game have tried to learn and apply Hogan's fundamentals in one form or another. However, in trying to adapt Hogan's puzzle to their own game, most golfers have come up with some valid questions about the man and his method.

"Why was the downswing plane aimed to the right of and shallower than the backswing plane?"

"How could he start his downswing by turning his hips and not hit the ball way left?"

"How could he play with a closed stance with his long clubs and still hit a fade?"

"How did he take the left side of the golf course out of play?"

"Why was his ball position so far forward?"

"How did he hit it so far for a little guy of only 135–140 pounds?"

"Why can't I feel that coiled 'elastic strip'[xii] feeling on my back-swing?"

"Why did he have that extra spike in the toe of each shoe?"

As students of golf and Hogan, we have answered these questions with research, analysis, testing, and the application of principles of mathematics and physics. The result is the *final missing piece* of Hogan's secret puzzle.

When all of these pieces are put in place, and the *final missing piece* is added, the puzzle is complete. You will have the answers to many, if not all, of your questions. After reading this book, the fundamentals in *Five Lessons* will make a lot more sense. You will understand why Hogan's swing looked the way it did and why his ball flight and sound were so different from his contemporaries. With this knowledge and some patience and hard work, you can apply Hogan's *missing piece* to your own golf game. It is for real; it has been tested; and golfers are already winning tournaments using this unique move.

The puzzle pieces are explained in detail in chapters 6–8 for those who enjoy studying the golf swing and the math and physics behind it.

If you haven't already skipped ahead for it, the *missing piece*—Hogan's one special move that makes everything in the puzzle fit—is revealed in the next chapter.

Chapter 5

The Missing Piece of Ben Hogan's Secret Puzzle

As mentioned in chapter 1, despite the popularity of *Five Lessons,* many students and instructors believe the man held back some vital information about his swing. They feel that Hogan detailed most of the puzzle pieces but did not disclose the final piece.

That is also our conclusion after studying Hogan's writing on the swing, working with elite amateurs and tour players, and extensively analyzing film footage and photographs of his swing. It becomes particularly evident that something is missing when we examine Hogan's discussion about the action of the hips, especially his lack of detail regarding something he felt was very important.

Like many golfers, I tried to incorporate some of Hogan's key fundamentals into my swing at a few points in my golf career, but they just didn't seem to work like they should. I couldn't see or feel the shift in the plane that Hogan describes in *Five Lessons* or understand why it was shallower on the downswing than on the backswing. The faster I turned my hips, the more the ball came off the toe, and it was usually a pull-hook left or a toe-tickling right shot.

Eventually, I rationalized this in a number of different ways that are common among golfers who have tried to adopt Hogan's method. "I could not practice as much as Hogan did," or "my wrists did not hinge as far as his," or "there was something that I just didn't understand." It didn't seem right that I couldn't grasp and perform a swing that was supposed to be the model for the world's most reliable swing, as described by the master himself.

I could understand how amateur golfers could not make Hogan's book and swing work for them. But I was a competent teaching professional, confident of my knowledge of the swing, and I was a good player. It didn't seem right that I could not figure out Hogan's puzzle.

After viewing hours of footage of Hogan's swing, however, I noticed that he was doing something amazingly different from what he taught in his book and from what we read in most modern golf instruction. After calling on my friends for their technical analysis and confirmation, I am now 100 percent convinced that Hogan did have "a secret," and that there was a "*final missing piece*" to his golf swing puzzle. When this piece was put in place, his entire book made total sense, and I could discard all of my rationalizations on why *Five Lessons* did not work for me or for many others.

Fig. 6 and 7 - Ben Hogan and the *missing piece*

If you have solid fundamentals, you too can incorporate the *missing piece* into your golf game. You can start to hit shots with the consistency that you have dreamed of, whether you are a professional, scratch golfer, or a mid-handicapper.

Your swing will feel completely different from anything you have ever done; this is not necessarily bad. Over the years you have probably tried many different swings, but all had the same basic feeling and the same unsatisfactory results. Maybe now is the time to try something that actually FEELS DIFFERENT.

Hogan led us to the water, but he did not let us drink. Hogan understood the action that would tie the pieces together, but he left the final piece for us to figure out.

The "secret" is out. All golfers can now take advantage of the *final missing piece* of Hogan's secret puzzle.

THE *MISSING PIECE* IS THE LATERAL MOVEMENT OF BEN HOGAN'S HIPS FORWARD AND OVER HIS LEFT LEG, PRIOR TO THE COMPLETION OF HIS BACKSWING.

The following explanation outlines key elements of the *missing piece* in more detail. As Hogan made his backswing, the majority of his weight was transferring to his left foot. This process continued until he had transferred about 80 percent of his weight to his left foot DURING HIS BACKSWING. The motion of Hogan's hips has always been regarded as the key element of his swing. Indeed, they did play a crucial role in moving his center of gravity over this foot. During his backswing, his hips moved laterally forward toward his left foot, while they turned clockwise at the same time. The forward movement of his hips began when his hands approached the waist-high position on his backswing (in Hogan's case the shaft was parallel to the ground at this point), and his hips completed this forward motion just PRIOR to the start of his downswing.

Several top instructors have correctly noted Hogan's lateral shift over the past 50 years. However, in all but two written pieces it was incorrectly identified as part of his downswing. In addition, Hogan's pivot has often been called a reverse pivot, a motion associated with high handicappers. Due to these and other factors, the true significance of Hogan's body motion has been overlooked.

Simply put, Hogan combined the lateral motion of his body WITH his backswing. This factor is very important because it fundamentally changes our understanding of Hogan's swing.

This lateral motion in Hogan's backswing is easily verified by viewing Clem Darracott's excellent video, *Ben Hogan: In Pursuit of Perfection,* which is available in VHS and DVD formats. The footage was shot with an eight-mm home movie camera on the practice range during the 1967 Masters. That was the year that 54-year-old Hogan electrified the galleries by shooting 30 on the back nine on Saturday. This gave him a stunning 66 and left him just two behind the leaders heading into the final round. However, a balky putter and the cumulative effect of Augusta National's hills on his weary legs finally did him in. A final round of 77 dashed his hopes for a miraculous win, but it was still good enough for a top ten finish.

As chronicled by Bill Fields in *Golf World*, Hogan described his Saturday back nine at the 1967 Masters to reporter Furman Bisher: "I think I played the best golf of my life on those last nine holes. I don't think I came close to missing a shot."[xvii]

In Darracott's video and in the swing sequence in the middle of this book, you can observe Hogan's left hip during his backswing. You will note how much of the background disappears behind his left hip as it moves forward laterally while he coils and takes the club back.

Most films of Hogan do not show this degree of lateral movement. However, most of the sequence shots of his swing were NOT taken while he competed or when he was preparing for competition. In my analysis of the limited available video footage of Hogan, it appeared that the post-accident Hogan showed a different swing to the camera than the swing that he employed when competing. The *missing piece* is most clearly seen in footage of Hogan's competitive swings.

The Simple Genius of Hogan's Move

By moving his center of gravity forward over the inside of his left foot during his backswing, Hogan accomplished three things:

1. He could start his downswing with an aggressive turn of the

25

hips and maximize the angular acceleration of his body and the clubhead.

2. He eliminated the left side of the golf course. By moving his weight and his left shoulder forward during his backswing, Hogan could then turn his hips and swing his arms as hard left as he wanted. The ball would not go left, because his left shoulder was farther forward than at address.

3. With his lateral forward motion completed during his backswing, Hogan developed a much more accurate and repeatable swing.

This last point is essential to understanding Hogan's move. In most traditional instruction, the key moves in the downswing are a forward movement of the hips, followed closely by a hip turn. This forward motion of the hips is the main factor in transferring the weight onto the left foot.

To work in proper sequence, these two motions have to be expertly timed. The two motions are so closely linked that in effect, they are closer to being one motion.

With his lateral forward motion completed during his backswing, Hogan separated the motions into two distinct moves that occurred at different times. In the first of these two distinct moves, his hips moved laterally on his backswing at the same time that they rotated clockwise to the 45-degree turned position he specifies in *Five Lessons*. Then he simply turned his hips to start his downswing.

By separating the lateral move of the hips and the counterclockwise turning of the hips to start the downswing, Hogan's swing was much easier to time and to move in sequence, and therefore to repeat.

Like a gyroscope, Hogan's body could rotate rapidly around an axis of rotation that was anchored at his left foot. The motion of his body ensured that the low point of the swing occurred in the same spot every time and that with correct, educated hand action he could achieve repeatable impact alignments (a flat or slightly bowed left wrist and straight left arm at impact) with every swing.

Why You've Struggled

In *Five Lessons*, Hogan stresses the importance of starting the downswing with the turning of the hips. In fact, he mentions it OVER 40 TIMES, so it was obviously important to him. However, most amateurs cannot master this critical move, and it's one of the main reasons they struggle with Hogan's teaching.

Most amateurs cannot get their weight over to their left side soon enough in the downswing. If the average golfer starts to turn his hips with his weight centered, he completely opens up the left side of the golf course because his center of gravity is behind the ball and his left shoulder may or may not get ahead of the ball. The tendency for an average player is to come over the top and pull the ball left; a better player will likely hit a hook. To counteract this tendency and to get the weight over the left foot earlier in the swing, better players will slide the hips forward at the beginning of the downswing before rotating them.

However, it is difficult to slide and then turn the hips repeatedly and accurately at the beginning of your downswing unless you have the coordination of a touring pro, and even then this will occasionally fail. It requires tremendous coordination in order to consistently move the center of mass forward when the hips are turning, so players stop turning their hips, and they tend to hold the clubface open to prevent the pull-hook. They begin to lay the face back and play a pull-slice.

By incorporating the *missing piece* into his swing, Hogan got his hips forward during his backswing. Once there, Hogan could start the downswing by turning his hips and move his body in perfect sequence for maximum power.

With this hip action, Hogan figured out a way for his body to produce repeatable alignments, a flat or slightly bowed left wrist and a straight left arm at impact, every time. This body motion allowed his hands to play a much lesser role. His body put him in a perfect position to hit the ball with power and precision.

Challenging Traditional Thinking

Over the past 40 years, it has become a fundamental of golf instruction that we must move on to the right side at the top of the backswing, then shift laterally at the start of the downswing. Is this wrong? No, it is simply different from the move Hogan made. Is Hogan's move easier? You'd better believe it. This is the beauty of Hogan's *missing piece*. It is not difficult to learn and perform, and it is far easier to sequence.

Arguably, the golf swing is one of the most difficult motions in sports. One of the reasons is the precision timing involved in the nearly simultaneous shift-and-turn movement of the hips that has become a staple of downswing instruction. Add self-imposed pressure and tension that creeps into everyone's game, and it becomes that much more difficult to move the body—which is moving very quickly to begin with—in the correct sequence. Hogan's move makes it much easier for average golfers to perform and feel the correct motions and then to execute them in the proper sequence.

Performing the *Missing Piece*

If you haven't tried it, now is the time to feel the correct motion and sequence of Hogan's move. Get into your setup position, standing with a club in front of a mirror, and follow this sequence:

1. Start your backswing by shifting a bit of your weight onto your right foot. (This little move or bump helps get your body moving and creates momentum.)

2. When your hands are waist high, start to move your hips forward toward your left foot, AS you start turning them in the backswing. Your head will automatically lower, but do not let it move forward with your hips.

3. Start your downswing by turning your hips counterclockwise, as soft or as hard as you want.

IT IS THAT SIMPLE, AND IT IS WHAT HOGAN ACTUALLY DID.

It's important to note that Hogan's swing blended rotation with a lateral move. As he turned on his backswing, his shoulders turned 90 degrees and his hips turned 45 degrees. In fact, while Hogan turned his body clockwise on his backswing, he simultaneously moved his hips laterally to the left. This is a simple move to perform. (You might try it a few times before reading further.) This is largely because it is easier to control the backswing, while the downswing is more of a reaction move. That is, the downswing involves a release of tension brought on by stretching our muscles in the backswing turn.

In the sequence of Hogan's swing, his hips turned clockwise on his backswing while they moved forward at the same time. He moved most of his weight over the inside of his left foot on his backswing. This put Hogan in a position to release the torque created by his backswing and move into the ball by turning his hips to the left, thus igniting a powerful sequence of motion through the ball.

This is important background for understanding the *missing piece.* To integrate the motion into your swing, here's all you have to remember:

1. BUMP.
   Bump your hips one inch backward.
2. TURN AND MOVE FORWARD.
   Turn your hips 45 degrees clockwise
   as you move over your left foot.
3. ROTATE.
   Rotate your hips counterclockwise
   to start your downswing.

BUMP   TURN AND MOVE   ROTATE

Fig. 8.

In other words, SHIFT a bit of your weight onto your right foot early in the backswing. Then, as you continue to TURN to the top, MOVE LATERALLY FORWARD over to the inside of your left

29

foot. The next move? Start your downswing by ROTATING your hips.

Hogan's sequence of motion simplified the timing of the swing. In an effort to make the swing even simpler, some readers might ask: "Why can't I just start with my weight over my left foot?" Well, you can. You will gain some accuracy but lose some power because you will not have created the same degree of momentum that starts with Hogan's bump backwards, towards his right foot. Your swing will also lack the balance and natural movement that gave Hogan's swing its grace, beauty, and power.

The question about starting with the weight on the left foot is a logical one because many golfers have done the classic drill of hitting balls with their feet together. In fact, most golfers naturally place the majority of their weight on their left foot in performing this drill. It's a great drill for getting rid of excess lateral movement and feeling the simplicity of the swing. Many golfers have perfected this drill to the point where they can hit shots that fly directly at the target with a little draw.

However, when they take their normal stance or move their feet even an inch apart, these golfers find that they cannot hit the ball with the same precision. A common question is "Why can I hit the ball crisply and accurately with my feet touching each other, but when I go back to my normal stance, I go back to my same lousy contact?"

This is because when you moved your feet apart, you went from a pure body pivot around your left leg to an incorrectly sequenced body pivot and a variable low point at impact. Poor contact and an inconsistent shot pattern are the net result. The *missing piece* in Hogan's swing provides the correct sequence of motion so that you can enjoy a combination of increased accuracy and power.

Finally, to the skeptics who will complain that the *missing piece* is based on pictures of a 54-year-old Hogan well past his prime, we would like to offer the following comments:

1. Clem Darracott's home movies of Hogan were taken four days before Hogan shot what he personally described as the best nine holes of golf he ever played, and Hogan said he never missed a shot in those nine holes. This statement is especially significant coming

from a golfer who was famous for saying he never hit more than two or three good shots a round.

2. Fred Gronauer was one of the dozen top pros interviewed by *Life* for the April, 1954 article on Ben Hogan's secret. He was a contemporary of Ben Hogan's, and his analysis of Hogan's swing was based on slow motion pictures of the swing from 1953, and probably even earlier. His depiction of Hogan's secret in 1954 (See figure 2, page 7) was ample proof that Gronauer was very observant and that he was familiar with Hogan's swing. His analysis of the secret was close, but incomplete, and this vital clue to the true secret was thus ignored for the ensuing 50 plus years. However, the picture of Gronauer's almost perfect demonstration of the *missing piece* is convincing proof that Ben Hogan was using this unique move in 1953, his greatest year ever.

3. We have never read anywhere that Hogan's backswing changed significantly since the early '50s. His putting and his eyesight declined, and his left leg may not have straightened after impact as quickly[xviii], but we are not aware of any written record of a decline or change in his pre-impact swing or his ball-striking ability.

Therefore, we feel confident that Hogan's swing at the 1967 Masters was still representative of the swing which made him a legend and created the "secret" controversy to begin with.

So there you have it: Hogan's secret revealed.

To help you understand the *missing piece* in greater detail, we have detailed the physics, math, and geometry behind it. We have provided an analysis of Hogan's swing in the following three chapters. These details are meant for serious students of the swing, avid fans of Hogan, and professional instructors. DO NOT FEEL THAT YOU HAVE TO UNDERSTAND THE NEXT THREE CHAPTERS IN ORDER TO USE THIS BOOK; YOU DO NOT.

If you have a clear understanding of what Hogan actually did, reinforced by pictures in this book of him using the *missing piece*, then you can start doing the drills immediately and begin fitting the *missing piece* into your own golf game today.

Chapter 6

Hogan's Fundamentals: The Puzzle Pieces in Detail

Before adding the *missing piece* to your golf swing, we recommend that you read or review *Five Lessons* because Hogan gave us most of the other pieces of his secret puzzle in this book. Hogan's views on the fundamentals are just as valid today as they were in 1957. In his book, Hogan articulated the fundamentals that he used to become the ultimate champion of his era. These fundamentals were a hit when they were first published in five installments of *Sports Illustrated*, and they evolved into the *Five Lessons* book.

The first fundamental and piece of the puzzle is the GRIP. Hogan's grip had the "V" of his left hand pointing toward his right eye, while the "V" of his right hand pointed toward his chin. In combination with the arching or bowing of his left wrist through the impact area, this created an open clubface alignment. This is definitely an antihook grip, and it is often cited as his true secret.

His FOOTWORK is the second puzzle piece which he described in great detail. Hogan stressed that the right foot should be perpendicular to the target line on all shots. By keeping his right foot in this position and maintaining the flex in the right knee on the backswing, Hogan limited hip turn to a maximum of about 45 degrees, which he considered ideal. (Note: As he got older and lost some flexibility, his right foot pointed more to the right so he could maintain his 45-degree hip turn).

Hogan also advocated that the left foot be turned open one-quarter turn or about 22 degrees. This made it easier to turn the hips counterclockwise on the downswing and to finish with the weight on the left foot. Hogan cautioned golfers against taking a stance that is too narrow, stating that the feet should be as wide as the shoulders with a five-iron and then widen or narrow according to the club being used.

The third puzzle piece is Hogan's ADDRESS ALIGNMENT, and this is one of the hidden pieces. His variable foot positions on page 125 of *Five Lessons* have caused countless thousands of readers to assume that his thighs, hips, and shoulders followed the alignment of his feet, and this is the way golf has been traditionally taught. If you want to hit a draw or hook, close your stance by drawing your right foot back from the target line; to hit a fade or slice, open your stance by drawing your left foot back from the target line.

However, Clem Darracott's video shows that Hogan did not do this. The footage shows that his thighs, hips, and shoulders are all aligned to the target no matter where his feet are pointing. Darracott noted that Hogan hit consecutive draws, fades, and straight shots with no noticeable change in his swing or body alignments. In *Five Lessons*, Hogan does not link foot position with initial alignment, but instead he uses the right foot's location to determine the amount of hip turn.

The fourth puzzle piece is the interaction of his ARMS during the swing. The drawing of Hogan's arms roped together is famous. With this vivid image he created a mental picture of the arms tied together and working in unison. Most of us have tried this briefly before discarding it. It felt restricting and tight. Without the *missing piece*, we needed to have our arms free to swing them out to the right after impact in order to save the shot by preventing the pull. With the addition of the *missing piece*, this arm connection to the body is now possible, and it makes a lot of sense. In fact, most of the puzzle pieces make a lot more sense when they are used in conjunction with the *missing piece*.

Piece number five is BALL POSITION. In *Five Lessons* it is very specific. Hogan said to locate the ball one-half to one inch back from his left heel for all normal shots. He stressed that ball position was constant, and it is very important to understand that this ball position is correct. When you try this it will likely feel too far forward, but with the *missing piece*, it will eventually feel natural.

Five Lessons goes into detail on two specific backswing points. Puzzle piece six is the WAGGLE as the bridge from address to the takeaway. Here Hogan points out that the waggle is a rehearsal for the type of shot being played. For piece number seven, Hogan teaches a BACKSWING SEQUENCE with the hands leading the shoulders, the shoulders leading the hips, and so on down to the feet. This is a significant change from the "one-piece" takeaway that he advocated in his earlier book, *Power Golf*.

Piece number eight is the DOWNSWING SEQUENCE, and it revolves around one main point: turning the hips counterclockwise. Hogan says a substantial amount of weight must be over the forward foot as the swing starts down. He also tells us that the hips are pivotal in the golf swing and that if they do not begin the downswing, the player will get out of position. The application of the *missing piece* makes all of this work.

The IMPACT description in *Five Lessons* revolves around the beautiful drawing of Hogan's arching or bowing left wrist and the use of the right arm. This insightful view of impact became a foundation for the teaching concepts of thousands of instructors, and this can be considered puzzle piece nine.

The tenth puzzle piece involves straightening the RIGHT ARM. Hogan did not straighten his right arm AT impact, but he allowed it to straighten THROUGH impact. In making his point, Hogan said he wished he had three right hands. Golfers plagued by a hook—which is accentuated by the right hand turning over—were confused by this image, and they questioned the soundness of Hogan's teaching. Nevertheless, proponents of a hands-oriented swing often quote this reference to his right hand and use it to justify a hands-controlled swing.

Finally, puzzle piece eleven is the SWING PLANE and Hogan's unique depiction of a rectangular pane of glass to show the ideal path of the club. Hogan FELT that the pane of glass moved lower and pointed more to the right as he started his downswing. (When the clubhead followed this imaginary image, it moved from inside the target line to outside the line.) When you apply the *missing piece*, it becomes much easier to understand the concept and feel the swing plane that Hogan FELT.

I recommend and challenge you to go back through *Five Lessons* and make notes on Hogan's fundamentals. If you haven't read it yet, get a copy. His fundamentals are clearly stated, sound, and critical to understanding the *missing piece*.

A Modern View

Now, let's take a look at Hogan's swing from my perspective as a teaching professional with access to state-of-the-art video analysis equipment and the benefit of 50 years of advancement in golf instruction. Two key characteristics of Hogan's swing remain unique today: his flat swing plane and the way he swung left through the ball.

At the top of Hogan's backswing, his hands are below his right shoulder—not directly below, but if you draw a line horizontally from the shoulder, the hands are below the line. Why? Hogan studied the swings of great batters in baseball. He believed there was a connection between how baseball players and golfers moved their hands and arms, especially the hand action required to make a free, full swing on a horizontal plane. (I've often had a mental image of Hogan standing in a hotel room in front of a mirror. With Valerie watching, he keeps going over this horizontal swing and the movement of his arms to the top.) Placing his hands and arms in this position contributed to his flat swing plane.

Hogan's arms also swung distinctively left through impact. At first sight, it appears almost exaggerated. Along with the forward-looking ball position, you would bet your life the ball would go quickly left or be hit so far out on the toe that the club would twist in his hand, but it did not. With the *missing piece*, Hogan's ball left the club face with a controlled trajectory and a sound that was Hogan's alone. We researched this movement until we completely understood it.

What we found is that most of Hogan's contemporaries swung their arms "down the line" or to the right after impact. Look at the swings of Claude Harmon Sr., Jackie Burke Jr., Vic Ghezzi, or most of his contemporaries, and you'll see that their arms move more inside-out or down the line through impact than Hogan's did. In *Five Lessons*, Hogan wrote about the club moving inside-out and the shallowing of the downswing plane, but he didn't discuss his arms swinging to the left or up the downswing plane after impact.

The movement of Hogan's arms to the left can be understood by observing his right arm. It does not straighten as quickly as most players'. This arm motion is best seen in *Five Lessons* on pages 97–99. Most of Hogan's peers straightened their right arm much sooner. If the right arm straightens out late and the body continues to rotate, the arms will appear to swing left through the impact area. But the

(Text continued on page 45)

35

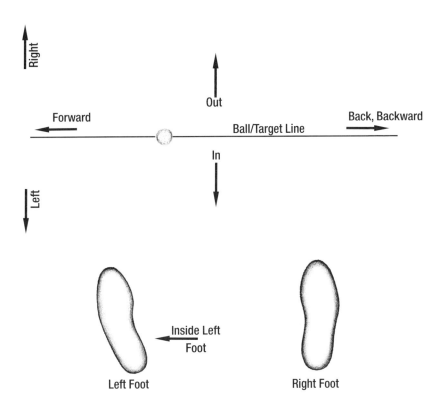

Fig. 9 - Definitions as used in this book

Fig. 10.

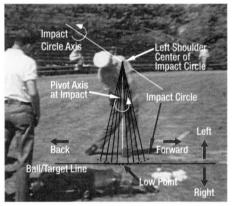

Fig. 11.

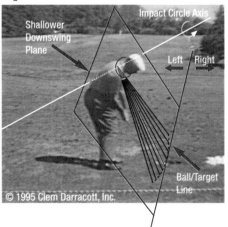

Fig. 12 - Definitions as used in this book

Backswing Plane

Actual
Shallower
Downswing Plane

Lowered Head
and Body

Backswing Plane

© 1995 Clem Darracott, Inc.

Fig. 13 - Ben Hogan's swing planes

38

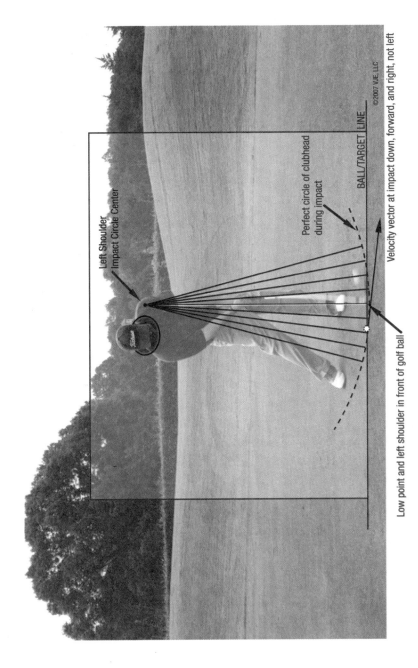

Left Shoulder
Impact Circle Center

Perfect circle of clubhead
during impact

Velocity vector at impact down, forward, and right, not left

BALL/TARGET LINE

©2007 VJE, LLC

Low point and left shoulder in front of golf ball

Fig. 14 - Ben Hogan's impact circle and shallower downswing plane

Fig. 15 - Ben Hogan and the *final missing piece* of his secret puzzle

Fig. 16 - A modern golf swing with the *missing piece* added

Fig. 17 - Ben Hogan's post-impact clubhead path

43

Before

After

©2007 VJE, LLC

Fig. 18 - A modern golf swing - before and after the *missing piece*

44

question still lingers: why did so many players do it differently?

Most swung inside-out as a defense against the ball starting left. They swung their arms away from the body and to the right to prevent a pull or pull-hook. Hogan did not. Through the *missing piece*, he took the left side out of play.

Hogan also wanted to take his hands out of the swing. When the pressure increases, what is the first thing to shake? The arms? The head? The legs? No, the hands. Hogan knew that he played better with less hand manipulation. With body motion, he built a golf swing that would stand up to tournament pressure because it was not dependent on precise hand action.

Hogan also played the ball farther forward in his stance with his short and mid irons than nearly all amateurs. A traditional golfer who plays the ball back tends to create a push, while this same golfer will pull a ball that is forward in his stance.

I wondered why Hogan didn't simply move the ball back in his stance to prevent the dreaded pull-hook. I puzzled over this many times before discovering the relationship between ball position and the *missing piece*. Hogan moved his center forward during the backswing, which moved his left shoulder farther forward at impact. This effectively moved the ball back in his stance.

Hogan returned to the ball with the left shoulder farther forward at impact than at address. This is a critical element based on precise geometry that has not been examined for decades. Like Hogan, Jack Nicklaus advocated playing the ball an inch off his left heel. One would think the rest of us would try the ball position favored by two of the greatest golfers in history. However, it simply did not work for the majority of golfers—at least until now.

Hogan also had an elegant and distinctively high finish. As a young golfer, I had a picture of Hogan in mid-follow-through: the arms fully extended, the wrist not yet recocked, and the clubhead a full 11 feet in the air. (See the full color picture next to page 12 of John Andrisani's *The Hogan Way* for one of the all-time great Hogan photos.)

Many amateurs suffer from another problem: they swing the club outside-to-in through the ball, which causes them to finish the swing with the club low and around them. They try desperately to attack the inside of the ball with their arms and hands, but their body motion sabotages this effort. The *missing piece* allows you to attack the ball from inside the target line and to finish with the club high like Hogan.

Hogan's leg action was also graceful and athletic with a wonderful flowing pace. Only a few of golf's elite players came close to matching his lovely leg movement. Today, down in the trenches with the single-digit to mid-handicaps, I see locked knees, jumping feet, wobbling hips—you name it.

This leg action was a major area of focus during my research into Hogan's swing. Now that I have incorporated the *missing piece* into my swing, my lower body motion resembles Hogan's—and the same goes for many of my students. Ten years ago, I would have paid you $10,000 (and I didn't have it) if you could have taught me to swing a golf club with a body motion like Hogan's. Now, through this book, you can learn to execute the body motion of Hogan at his very best.

Finally, there are two interesting questions regarding Hogan's swing that have gone unanswered for all of these years: "Why have I never felt the "elastic strip" power in my backswing that Hogan talks about on page 91 of *Five Lessons*?" and "Why did he have that extra spike in the front toe of each shoe?"

To feel the stored elastic strip power, take your normal stance at setup, then turn your shoulders the standard 90 degrees, while turning your hips 45 degrees. If you are like me, you will feel a little stretching, but not a lot. I could never feel the tension he was talking about. Next, make the same turn, but get most of your weight over the inside of your left foot while keeping your right foot fully on the ground. Now you can feel the tremendous stored stretching power Hogan outlined in his book. It is that simple.

The extra spike also results from the *missing piece*. Hogan advocated more than 40 times in *Five Lessons* that you start your downswing by turning your hips. But where does the force to do this come from? It starts with your right foot, specifically the inside edge or instep of your right foot and then your right toe.

To demonstrate this, make the same turn that you made in the elastic strip example, but shift ALL of your weight onto your left foot, with your right foot slightly off the ground. Now try to make a rapid counterclockwise hip turn to start your downswing. It is very difficult to do. You can either turn your shoulders and torso to make your hips rotate, or use the muscles in your left leg to start the rotation, and both are VERY WEAK moves.

Now, go to the top of the backswing position (90-degree shoulder rotation and 45-degree hip rotation) and place 80 percent of your weight on your left leg and 20 percent on your right leg. If you push off INCORRECTLY by using your right HEEL, your hips will try to rotate further clockwise. However, if you push off first with your right instep and then your right toe, you create a tremendously sound mechanical linkage to start a counterclockwise rotation of the hips. This is the "chain action"[xix] or "ground-up" start of the golf swing that so many old-time golf teachers advocated and that Hogan used so effectively. It creates a large rotational force on the hips, with very little lower back stress, and it is probably why Hogan could hit so many balls with no recorded history of back problems.

Largely on his own, Hogan used his intellect and work ethic to piece together his brilliant motion. Today, the best players mainly draw on the experience and knowledge of excellent golf instructors to implement changes.

Hogan also dressed for golf better than many of us dress for church. He cared about how he looked on the course and the image he projected. Hogan was a man's man, and this is one reason we are still enamored with him.

Hogan was an intense man. He even looked at the golf ball with resolve. You can see it in videos of his practice sessions. There's no mistaking that he is determined to be in control of that golf ball. It is humbling to watch the intense, almost hypnotic state with which he concentrates, and that is just on video. I can only imagine what it was like to watch him in person.

As golfers, how could we not all follow his lead? How could we not follow his advice with the golf swing?

Well, the reason was that IT DID NOT WORK FOR MOST OF US! At least not until now.

Chapter 7

Why It Works: The Geometry, Math, and Physics of the Missing Piece

Many golfers, instructors, and golf theorists use video as their primary means of exploring and understanding the complex motions that occur in the golf swing. Video is an important tool, but as we explore the complexities of the swing, it is even more important to reconcile what we THINK we see with the basic laws of science.

The amazing power produced by some golf swings seems mysterious until the science of motion is properly applied. Hogan probably never tried to understand these laws, but the swing he dug out of the dirt in Texas used them in their most efficient form. We can also apply these laws to our golf swings, but if we want to understand the physics behind the *missing piece*, we must first acquaint ourselves with some of the laws of physics.

To begin, we must define and understand the two different axes of rotation which apply to Hogan's *missing piece*, as well as the different terms and directions which will apply throughout this book. These are identified in the images on pages 36 and 37.

Hogan's *missing piece* involves the rotation of a mass around an axis. To understand the secret we must understand the concept of body mass and where this mass is located relative to the axis of rotation, which we refer to in this book as the PIVOT AXIS. For humans, the mass is basically the body weight. (For further discussion of mass and weight in the English system of measurement, see page 12 of *System Dynamics* by Ogata or a similar engineering textbook.)

The location of the pivot axis is not as readily measurable. The mathematically complete way to locate this axis involves the integration of many loosely coupled, nonrigid masses into an instantaneous solution. Likewise, the calculation of the exact center of gravity involves an integral solution that is valid only for one particular instant of time and one particular arrangement of body parts and golf club parts.

Fortunately, we don't need to know the precise location of the center of rotation or the center of gravity. WE ONLY NEED TO

UNDERSTAND THAT THE CLOSER THE CENTER OF GRAVITY IS TO THE AXIS OF ROTATION, THE MORE ANGULAR ACCELERATION WE CAN GENERATE WITH THE SAME APPLIED FORCE. (Note again that the terms center of mass and center of gravity can be used interchangeably.) At the instant the downswing starts, the entire weight of the golfer can be treated as if it were located at the center of gravity of the body.

What this means in the golf swing is simple and very important: the closer the center of gravity is to the pivot axis at the top of the swing (the start of the downswing), the faster the entire body can be accelerated by the available muscular forces during the downswing.

As applied to the golf swing, more angular acceleration means a faster body rotation and faster arms and hands in the chain action swing that Hogan describes in *Five Lessons*. This increases clubhead speed, which directly increases distance.

When analyzing Hogan's swing and his *missing piece*, it is necessary to understand two concepts: the LOW POINT and the IMPACT CIRCLE.

1. The left shoulder position at impact determines the low point of the golf swing and the relationship between ball position and the actual divot.

2. At the point of impact and a foot or so on each side of this point, the clubhead is traveling on a plane in a perfect circle, the impact circle. The center of this circle is the left shoulder, and the radius of the circle is the combined length of the extended left arm and the club itself.

This impact circle has its own axis of rotation, the IMPACT CIRCLE AXIS, and this axis is totally different from the PIVOT AXIS, although they are closely interrelated. The impact circle axis passes through the left shoulder and is perpendicular to the plane of the impact circle. The true radius of Hogan's impact circle is a line from his left shoulder (at impact) to a point in front of his ball (the low point of his swing). For Ben Hogan, the axis of his impact circle intersects the ground at a point approximately five feet behind his left foot, when he is set up with a driver. This axis is only applicable during that microscopic instant of time when the club moves through the ball at impact, but it is very real and the impact circle itself is easily identifiable on a V1 or similar video analysis system.

Hogan's pivot axis intersects the ground at his left foot, and basically follows his left leg. This pivot axis is not at a constant angle with the ground, but rather this angle varies throughout the downswing and forward swing. Hogan's center of gravity at impact was critical in determining his golf ball's initial direction (see chapter 9), because it was ON his pivot axis and precisely located his left shoulder in front of the golf ball. These two distinct axes of rotation are shown in figures 11 and 12 on page 37, and these terms will be used to identify the two axes throughout the book.

An analysis of Hogan's swing reveals several important components that resulted from incorporating the *missing piece* into his approach to striking a golf ball.

First, when Hogan set up to the ball, his center of gravity was exactly between his feet and "closer to his heels than his toes,"[xix] as he wrote in *Five Lessons*. This information provides a precise location for his center of gravity at the start of his swing. A vertical line drawn from the front of his heel would pass through his center of gravity, when looking down the line.

On his backswing, Hogan's golf club traveled beneath the imaginary inclined pane of glass shown on page 78 of *Five Lessons*. At the end of the backswing Hogan's head was almost two inches lower than at setup, and he then began his downswing on a shallower plane than his backswing. This initially shallower downswing plane was featured in *Five Lessons* and was a key component of Hogan's swing. It was a direct result of his use of the *final missing piece*.

Hogan's pivot axis was anchored in his left foot and extended upward, approximately following his left leg. This pivot axis was basically the same left leg downswing axis that is taught in classic golf instruction. The important difference between what Hogan actually did and what is traditionally taught is the timing of the weight transfer to the left leg.

Hogan's unique weight transfer created a look in his swing that many called a reverse pivot. In fact, Hogan moved his center of gravity onto his pivot axis, and his perfect balance proved that he never moved his weight backward during his downswing. He simply performed this weight transfer at a different time than anyone else— during his backswing, not at the start of his downswing.

What Moving His Center of Gravity Onto His Pivot Axis Did for Hogan

Moving his center of gravity onto his pivot axis accomplished several key things for Hogan.

1. From a physics standpoint, it increased Hogan's ability to rotate, because the closer the center of his mass was to his pivot axis, the faster he could rotate his body.

2. It ensured that the low point of his swing (his left shoulder) was in front of or even with the golf ball. From this position, Hogan would not have to worry about his ball starting left (more on this in chapter 9). His arms could now go left as fast as he wanted, as long as his EDUCATED HANDS maintained their correct impact alignments through impact (the left wrist flat or bowed and the right wrist bent).

3. It allowed his arms to stay close to his body during the swing. By having his center of gravity on his pivot axis, Hogan did not have to manipulate his hands and arms to keep the ball from going left. If his left shoulder had not been in front of or even with the ball at impact, Hogan would have needed to extend his arms to the right, away from his body, in order to hit most of his shots—a move that most of his contemporaries found necessary. Also, the closer the arms remain to the rotating body, the faster the body can rotate. The best example is a twirling figure skater: if she holds her arms out from her body and then brings them tight to her torso, her rotation speeds appreciably.

4. Finally, it gave Hogan his elegant body motion. Keep in mind that the rotation of an object about an axis that does not go through its center of gravity will create wobble. In a golf swing, wobble can be seen in the form of rotational problems such as stalling hips, excessively bowed knees after impact, aching backs and necks, and bodies that stop rotating.

The math and physics behind the *missing piece* is based on the work of Sir Isaac Newton in his book *Mathematical Principles of Natural Philosophy* in 1687. The formula for Newton's Second Law (for rotational motion) is on the next page, followed by the math and the hands-on models. Remember, you don't have to understand any of this to use the *missing piece* in your golf game.

Newton's Second Law (for rotational motion)

(angular acceleration)=(sum of torques) / (moment of inertia)

The formula for this is: $\alpha = \dfrac{\xi T}{J_c}$

where:
$\quad \alpha$ = angular acceleration
$\quad \xi T$ = sum of torques available to rotate the object
$\quad J_c$ = moment of inertia of object
$\quad CC^1$ = axis of rotation through center of mass (ideal)

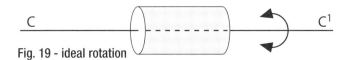

Fig. 19 - ideal rotation

When the above object is rotated about its center of mass, the above formula applies, and maximum angular acceleration is achieved. However, when this same object is rotated about an axis (xx^1) which does not go through its center of mass, the following formula now applies:

$$\alpha = \dfrac{\xi T}{J_x} = \dfrac{\xi T}{J_c + mR^2}$$

where:
$\quad$ R = distance new axis is from CC^1
$\quad$ m = mass of object
$\quad XX^1$ = new axis of rotation (inefficient)
$\quad J_x$ = moment of inertia about axis XX^1

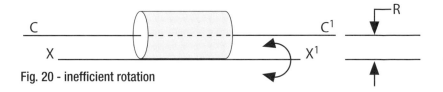

Fig. 20 - inefficient rotation

In this formula, J_x is the sum of all moments of inertia of the object, $(J_x = J_c + mR^2)$ and R is the distance the center of mass is from the new axis of rotation.

52

Applied to golf, the formula expressed in figure 19 shows that Hogan's ability to accelerate his body was maximized because his center of gravity was directly on his pivot axis (approximately his left leg.) By shifting his weight forward during his BACKSWING, he could then start his downswing with a powerful and immediate counterclockwise turn of his hips and create maximum angular acceleration (clubhead speed).

His tremendous power ALSO came from the fact that he could IMMEDIATELY start his downswing by rotating his hips. He did not have to wait for the forward or lateral shift of his weight over his left foot, as is required in most conventional golf swings. Hogan's power did NOT come from any significant linear motion toward the target during his downswing.

According to this second formula, maximum acceleration occurs when the center of gravity is located exactly on the pivot axis (R=0). Also, as the center of gravity moves away from this axis (as shown in figure 20), the angular acceleration decreases as the square of the distance from the axis, not linearly. Even a small amount of off-center rotation results in a substantial reduction in angular velocity and potential clubhead speed.

If you add legs to the above objects, you can create several rotational scenarios. In Figure 21, a less skilled golfer will start his downswing by turning about axis CC^1 or somewhere forward toward axis XX^1. This results in a power loss due to a reduced rate of angular acceleration.

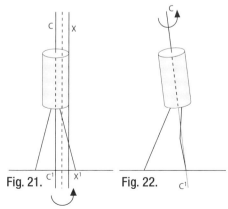

Fig. 21.   Fig. 22.

If this golfer rotates about CC^1 he will not get the full effect of the "elastic strip" coiling and will likely swing "over the top" and the ball will be pulled left or sliced right. If he rotates about an axis forward from CC^1, he will not be rotating his body mass efficiently about his pivot axis. He will create an imbalance or wobble (figure 28, page 58), and his angular acceleration will be greatly reduced.

A low-handicap amateur or accomplished professional golfer will move his weight forward and then turn, and his center of gravity will be as shown in figure 22, a position similar to Hogan's. This move requires a lot of coordination to do it the same every time, and by the time the accomplished golfer has moved his weight forward, Hogan would have already started his hip turn and be well into his downswing.

A second and more important result of this vastly different weight shift is the movement of most of his weight over his left foot and onto his pivot axis, which is his left leg. With Hogan, this point was very precise because his ball position was always the same distance from his left foot. With the center of his mass on his pivot axis, Hogan would always return to impact with the left shoulder farther forward than it was at address. This eliminated Hogan's toe shots, pulls, and the need for the arms to separate from the body; and it gave him confidence that the ball would not go left.

This forward weight shift and its unique timing gave Hogan the FEELING that he had a separate downswing plane that was shallower and aimed to the right of the target line.

In fact, what Hogan ACTUALLY did was different. He was quite correct in saying that his downswing plane was shallower than his backswing plane. However, the downswing plane was NOT aimed to the right of the target line. (This would have caused his arms to swing out to the right, like other players.) In fact, Hogan's clubhead approached the ball from inside the target line, squared at impact, and then moved back inside the target line. If his downswing plane had been aimed to the right of the target line, the clubhead would have traveled outside the target line after impact.

Also, sequence pictures such as those on pages 38 and 55 clearly show that Hogan's head was almost two inches lower on his downswing than at address; this is clear evidence of a shallower downswing plane. Similar sequence pictures show that his clubhead did not break the shallower downswing plane after impact, confirming the alignment of the backswing and downswing planes. (Refer to figure 17)

The physics and feel behind this center of gravity shift can be demonstrated with some common household items and the step-by-step instructions at the end of this chapter.

Finally, the figures below and on the next page, and the math in the appendix on pages 87 and 88 explain why Hogan referred to the downswing plane as flatter or "shallower" than his backswing plane. As can be easily seen in three different pictures in this book (figures 13, 24 and 25), Ben Hogan's head and body is lower at the top of the swing than at set-up. This lowering has two components, one from the upper body and the other from the lower body, and when these are added together, the total represents the distance Hogan's head and body actually lowered during his backswing.

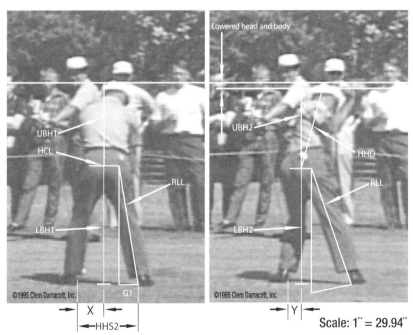

Fig. 23 - Hogan's triangles at setup   Fig. 24 - Hogan's triangles at the top

Scale: 1″ = 29.94″

The scaled lowering in figure 24 is **1.95″** (.065″ x 29.94″) and in figure 25 it is **2.09"** (.092″ x 22.685″) while the calculated value from the math on pages 87 and 88 is **1.97″**. These are remarkably close, and they confirm the accuracy of both the scaling and the

55

math calculations. Variables such as camera lens distortion, scaling accuracy, picture quality, and the estimated location of his hip joints all have a slight effect on the resulting calculations, and anything under one half of an inch would have been an acceptable variance.

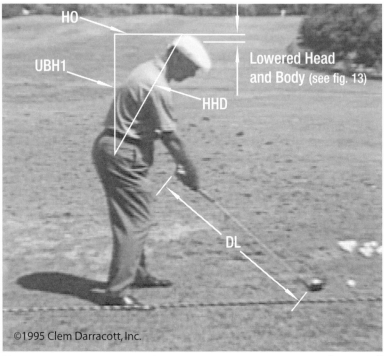

Fig. 25 - Hogan's upper body triangle at setup   Scale: 1″ = 22.685″

The basic premise for the math calculations is that the right leg length (RLL) and the hip-joint-centerline to top-of-head distances (HHD) are both constant. Since the right foot is still on the ground, and the right knee flex has not appreciably changed, the right leg is basically the same length. However the top of the right leg has moved forward and away from the ball as the hips turned 45 degrees and moved forward approximately four and a half inches, and this created a three-dimensional math puzzle. Likewise, the hip-joint-centerline to top-of-head measurement along the spine did not change, as can be seen in figure 13. Hogan's head lowered but did not move forward with his hips, and this created a slight spine tilt away from the ball and a second three dimensional math puzzle.

56

At set-up, the right leg length and hip-to-head measurements are the diagonals of two different two-dimensional triangles. However, when the hips move forward and turn during the backswing, these two constant dimensions each become the diagonal of a three dimensional right rectangular prism, and the math is based on this change. (See pages 87 and 88)

The reduced height of these prisms is the cause of the lowered, sitting-down look that is often used to describe Ben Hogan's downswing. This look is NOT what generated Hogan's powerful and accurate swing; rather, it is the end result of his incorporation of the *missing piece* into his swing.

This is the math behind the shallower downswing plane: When Hogan added the *missing piece* to his swing, it automatically created this new downswing plane, and it worked wonders for him. It can also work for you.

Demonstrating the Physics behind the Missing Piece

The physics and feel of this center of gravity shift can be demonstrated with a common wire coat hanger, a golf ball, a felt-tip pen, a sheet of copy paper, and eight inches of duct tape.

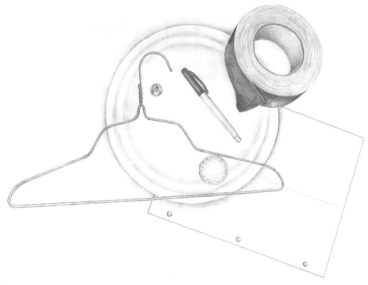

Fig. 26.

Straighten the hanger as shown, tape the ball between the wires, and hold it as shown in figure 27. The coat hanger represents the pivot axis, and the golf ball is the golfer's center of gravity. Now, hold the straightened hook of the coat hanger in your left hand and rapidly rotate the model using your right hand. Notice how easily you can perform this rotation. This is a model of what Hogan felt when he rotated his hips to start his downswing. By minimizing angular inertia (i.e., imbalance or wobble), he could achieve maximum angular acceleration.

FAST & SMOOTH

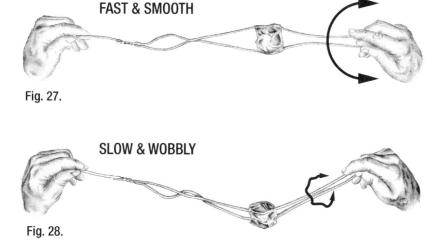

Fig. 27.

SLOW & WOBBLY

Fig. 28.

Now, bend the coat hanger so that the ball is two to three inches off-center (figure 28). Rotate the model again and notice how much harder the coat hanger is to rotate and how much slower it turns with the same amount of force. Note the imbalance or wobble you feel when rotating the model. This is the result of a non-zero R in the formula on page 52. This is what most golfers experience when starting their downswing.

Next, you can create a model of the shifted and shallower downswing plane that Hogan FELT when he started his downswing. Take a standard paper plate and draw a light line from the edge to the center of the plate. Next, draw two small dots on this line—one at the edge to represent the low point of the golf club's arc and the second two-thirds of the distance from the edge dot to the center to represent the center of gravity of the golfer.

Now draw a line down the middle of a sheet of plain copy paper, and place a dime on this line, in the center of the paper. Hold the plate at an angle, with the edge dot on the back side of the dime, as shown in figure 29. This represents the backswing pane of glass from *Five Lessons*.

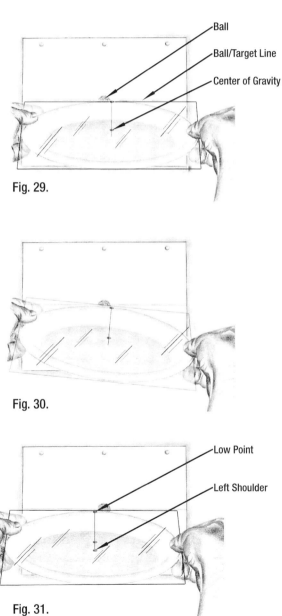

Fig. 29.

Fig. 30.

Fig. 31.

If this plate were covered with a square pane of glass, the bottom edge of this glass would lie on the line on the paper (ball/target line).

Next, move the middle mark (center of gravity) forward by one-half inch and lower it one-quarter inch, while keeping the edge of the plate on the back side of the dime. The dime represents the ball, and it has not moved, so the downswing plane must shift. Note in figure 30 how the new plate position is pointing to the right relative to its initial position, and also observe how it is at a shallower angle relative to the tabletop.

This is the downswing plane that Hogan FELT and described in his book. The plane shifted to the right automatically when he shifted his center of gravity over the inside of his left foot and onto his pivot axis, prior to the completion of his backswing. It also became shallower because his center of gravity was lower than at setup. This feeling gave him confidence that he could consistently hit the inside of the golf ball.

What Ben Hogan ACTUALLY Did

Draw a third dot in the middle of the plate. This represents the left shoulder at impact. Start with the plate on the dime as in figure 29. Next, move the plate forward so it is in front of the dime and lower it one-quarter inch, while keeping it lined up with the ball/target line (figure 31). Hogan's head and his center of gravity were almost two inches lower (figure 24), and this created the shallower downswing plane that he actually swung on.

His arms swung to the left after impact (see figure 17) and his clubhead stayed beneath the downswing plane. These moves were evidence that he did not actually swing on a downswing plane that was aimed to the right, but rather on a shallower version of his original backswing plane. Also, notice that the dot on the edge of the plate (low point) and the center dot (left shoulder) are lined up and in front of the dime (golf ball). This insured that his low point and the bottom of his divot were in front of the ball and that he contacted the ball when his club was travelling down, forward, and to the right at impact, never left. His use of the *missing piece* made this happen automatically.

60

Chapter 8

Examining Some Key Points in Hogan's Swing Mechanics

Before we move further into applying the *missing piece* to your game, it's important that we look at a few key details of Hogan's distinctive swing to ensure we understand the reasoning behind his swing mechanics.

Many golfers struggled with Hogan's teaching on page 125 of *Five Lessons* that we always play the ball an inch inside the left heel. Without the *missing piece*, playing the ball this far forward felt awkward. It was also difficult to hit the inside quadrant of the ball, and the varying lengths of our golf clubs made consistent impact elusive.

Hogan wanted the swing to feel the same every time. If he were to set up with the left foot in a different position relative to the ball for each club, he would have a different feeling at the top of his swing on nearly every shot. When Hogan moved his center of gravity to his left leg, the ball was perfectly placed for the same attack on the ball from inside the target line every time. It also allowed him to accurately control divot depth because the low point was always the same distance in front of the ball.

Hogan was also adamant about turning the hips counterclockwise to start the downswing. We have all tried this move without shifting our center of gravity, and the results are usually poor: either the ball goes left, or we hit it on the toe of the club and the ball flies high and right.

We have been out of sequence when following the instructions from *Five Lessons* because nowhere in the book did he explain exactly how and when to get your weight over your left foot.

As we've discussed, one of the key points of the *missing piece* is that Hogan moved his center of gravity over the inside of his left foot DURING his backswing. With this important move complete, Hogan started his downswing by simply turning his hips. I think that's why Hogan stressed turning the hips in *Five Lessons*; it was easy for him. Without the *missing piece*, however, it was difficult if not impossible for most of us.

Hogan's sequence of motion ensured that at impact the center of his mass was rotating around the pivot axis of his left leg. This also placed his left leg in a near-vertical position in front of the ball. The low point of his swing was always in front of the ball. With the *missing piece* and solid fundamentals, you can also get into these same positions in the proper sequence.

I always admired how Hogan kept his arms close to his body and swung left up the inclined plane after impact. If your center of gravity is behind the ball, you may hit the ball as far off the toe as you ever have. But with the center of your mass properly placed forward on your pivot axis, you can swing left with your arms as fast as you wish, and you will still be able to consistently find the sweet spot of the club. Of course, this depends on maintaining your spine angle and the correct sequence of movement, which are integral parts of an effective swing. When most mid- to high-handicap players try to swing hard, they disrupt their timing and get out of position by starting the downswing with the upper body instead of starting it from the ground up.

Most of Hogan's contemporaries moved their arms out and away from their bodies during the downswing. They swung the sweet spot of the club from inside-out or down-the-line on their forward swing. Viewed from down the line, the club exited ABOVE the left shoulder. They did this because their center of gravity was still between their feet and their left shoulder was not moving forward. They were great athletes, and they figured out how to attack the ball in the best way they could.

Hogan's club exited BELOW the left shoulder. Hogan's arm swing resulted from his center of gravity being over the inside of his left foot at the beginning of his downswing. This also allowed Hogan to lower—or shallow out—his plane angle for his downswing. His club approached the ball from inside the target line, met the ball squarely on the target line, and then moved back inside the line after impact. Every golfer needs to learn the body motion that creates the FEELING of this shifted plane if he wants to hit powerful and accurate shots consistently.

The shift in Hogan's swing plane occurred as he moved most of his weight over his left foot during the backswing. To prove this to yourself, go to the top of your swing with all your weight on your right leg. Now, if you simply turn your hips to start the downswing, a plane shift exactly OPPOSITE from Hogan's will occur: You will swing from outside to inside the target line. This is the way nearly all mid- to high-handicap amateurs play golf.

We have emphasized the left leg, but the right leg is also very important. Hogan maintained the flex in his right knee, which helped to create the unique look and consistency of his golf swing. In the early stages of his backswing, Hogan displayed an almost imperceptible backward movement of his right leg, then a very pronounced movement forward. At the end of his backswing his right leg was angled much more forward than at address, as shown in the pictures on pages 40 and 41. He started his backswing with a VERY SMALL backward shift of his center of gravity in order to create fluidity and momentum, then moved it drastically forward before completing his backswing. This was his final secret.

With longer clubs, Hogan would bump his right hip and right leg slightly more than with his short irons. But with all of his clubs, he moved his center of gravity backward only briefly and minimally before moving it forward. When his club was horizontal on his backswing, Hogan began moving his center of gravity to the same forward location on every shot. (This underscores the importance of positioning the ball an inch inside the left heel for every shot.) HOGAN'S RIGHT LEG ANCHORED HIS CENTER OF GRAVITY EARLY IN THE SWING, AND THE LEFT FOOT INDICATED WHERE TO TAKE HIS CENTER OF GRAVITY AT THE TOP. This is clearly seen in the right leg's increased angle at the top of the swing.

Fig. 32.

The positioning of Hogan's right arm at impact also provides us with some important clues about the *missing piece*. At impact and for a few inches afterwards, Hogan's right elbow and right wrist remained bent. His right arm didn't straighten until the club was nearly parallel with the ground after impact.

The action of Hogan's right arm was dependent on his lower body. In his words, he had a "chain action"[xx] swing, meaning it started from the ground up. This gave him an unbelievably consistent shot pattern and control of the clubface and clubhead path through impact.

With Hogan's weight forward and his left shoulder in front of the ball, his right arm did not have to straighten to save the shot because his body was in the proper position to support his arm swing. If he had not been in this position, he would have needed his right arm to straighten much earlier to keep the ball from going left, just as many of his contemporaries did. So Hogan's right arm action was based primarily on his center of gravity shifting to his pivot axis and over the inside of his left foot.

Without this "ground up" sequence that begins with a forward center of gravity, the average player's right arm has to be used mainly to keep the ball from going left and only secondarily for power. This is why the average player's right arm is fairly straight just after impact, when the shaft is at about a 45-degree angle to the body. It is a losing battle. If you do not use the *missing piece*, your body motion will be incorrectly sequenced and therefore your arms will not work efficiently.

When Hogan put his key fundamentals in place after the car accident, he no longer had to worry about hitting the ball left. The pulls and pull-hooks of his early career were but bad memories. In the next chapter, we'll discuss how the *missing piece* can also provide you with the same peace of mind and confidence.

BUMP

TURN AND MOVE   ROTATE

Fig. 33.

Chapter 9

How Hogan Took the Left Side of the Course Out of Play

When Hogan added the *missing piece* to his golf swing, he took the left side of the golf course out of play. This is an important accomplishment for a golfer of any ability level, but especially for a touring pro. A professional whose misses can go both right and left will not need nearly as much shelf space for trophies as the pro whose misses are confined to one side of the course. It is even more important to eliminate the LEFT side because he will no longer fear the dreaded pulls and pull-hooks when faced with knee-deep rough, an out of bounds fence, or six lanes of traffic along the left side of the fairway.

Perhaps the best example of Hogan's ability to take the left side out of play occurred during his historic victory in the 1953 Open Championship at Carnoustie and his play of the sixth hole.

The fairway on the par-five sixth hole is divided into two landing areas by a pair of deep bunkers. However, the left fairway is very narrow. There is only a 20-30-yard opening between the bunkers and the out of bounds fence that frames the entire left side. With the equipment available in 1953, Hogan didn't have the option of trying to carry the bunkers.

In the first three rounds, Hogan played conservative drives to the right fairway, but this route created a difficult second shot and made it impossible to reach the green in two.

In the final round, however, Hogan chose to go left of the bunkers to give himself the best possible angle into the green. Despite the danger in aiming for the narrow strip between the bunkers and out of bounds, Hogan hit a powerful drive that started down the out of bounds line and faded safely back into the fairway. He hit the green in two, made birdie, and went on to win by three shots. With the stakes so high in his quest to win three majors in the same year, this was arguably one of the best drives in major championship history.

To commemorate this phenomenal display of shot-making under the pressure of trying to make history, that narrow stretch of Scottish fairway was dubbed "Hogan's Alley," and his steely nerves throughout the tournament earned him the affectionate nickname "the Wee Icemon."

(Note: There are two versions to this story: the well-known tale in which Hogan went left all four days and the one told by James Dodson in his book *Ben Hogan: An American Life* in 2004. Dodson's version is based on recollections of Hogan's caddy Cecil Timms as told to R&A historian Donald Steel.)

Hogan took the left side out of play by shifting his body and left shoulder forward, along the shallower downswing plane, and toward the target. He did this precisely and accurately during his backswing. When he made this move, he changed the relative positioning of his center of gravity, his left shoulder at impact, and the golf ball. This had the effect of moving the ball back and up the shallower downswing plane, along the arc of the impact circle (figure 34) .

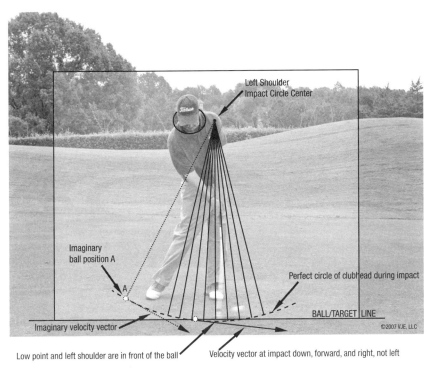

Fig. 34 - The impact circle

This created a clubhead path (velocity vector) at impact that went down, forward, and right, never left. It is still possible to hit the ball left if the clubface is closed at impact (the force vector is left at impact) but a reasonably accomplished golfer with correctly working hands can minimize this possibility. By shifting his center of gravity over the inside of his left foot as part of his backswing, Hogan created a swing geometry that was always the same in relation to his left foot and a left shoulder that was always in front of—or even with—the golf ball. Even with this forward ball position, he knew his ball would always start straight or slightly right of the target.

The concept of the velocity vector can be difficult to grasp. To help understand the velocity vector and its impact on the initial ball direction, imagine that the ball is drastically moved back and up the circle to point A in the impact circle in figure 34. Assuming that you could hit the ball in this location, it is easy to see that the only place the ball could go is down, forward, and to the right. It would be almost impossible for the ball to start left. The same thing happens at the bottom of the impact circle during a normal swing, but on a much smaller scale.

It is important to stress that the downswing plane Hogan mentions in *Five Lessons* was half feeling and half fact. It was definitely shallower than his backswing plane (see figure 13, page 38), but it did not shift to the right, even though it FELT that way to Hogan and it will FEEL that way to you. His downswing plane was actually a shallower version of his backswing plane, and it was aligned with the ball/target line. Videos of his swing show this to be true. His arms and clubhead never broke this shallower plane; they always stayed below it. His arms worked left after impact, staying beneath this downswing plane, and rotated perfectly around his left shoulder and impact circle axis during the few milliseconds that the club was at the bottom of its arc (see figure 17).

This chapter, like most of this book, assumes that you are familiar with the fundamentals of *Five Lessons*. Hogan's book is still the definitive source for his fundamentals. If you find yourself struggling, review these fundamentals and the *missing piece* motions described earlier in the book, and you'll likely get back on track.

The *missing piece* will give you tremendous confidence on the course.

Knowing that you've taken one side out of play will allow you to be more relaxed, but also to be more aggressive in plotting your line of attack on each fairway and green. The best golfers in the world play like this, and now it is possible for you to do so, IF you are willing to put in the work required to learn and engrain the *missing piece*. The next chapter will start you on that journey.

Fig. 34.1 - Ben Hogan's impact circle

Chapter 10

Drills for Learning the Final Missing Piece

Hogan's *missing piece* is radically different from the modern swing that has been taught for the past few decades. Golfers have been instructed to load their right side by allowing the majority of their weight to move to their right foot on the backswing. The *missing piece* is the complete opposite, with most of the weight moving to the left foot on the backswing.

To learn the *missing piece* and engrain the new motion, you've got some work to do. Learning a motor skill takes many, many repetitions until the new motion becomes patterned on your brain. While you are doing these drills, you will become consciously competent in your new motion—you're thinking about it. If you diligently practice these drills, you will eventually become unconsciously competent—you can perform the *missing piece* without thinking about it. That's where you want to get so that on the course, you can just swing away and play the game.

It takes commitment, time, and certainly some hard work. These drills will help you learn the mechanics of Hogan's *missing piece*. The fun that you have hitting powerful and accurate shots on the course will be in proportion to the work you put in on these drills, most of which you can do at home, at the office, or just about anywhere.

If you need some inspiration, think about how hard Hogan worked on his game. As role models go, you couldn't do any better.

Drill 1 – Ensuring Consistent Stance and Ball Position

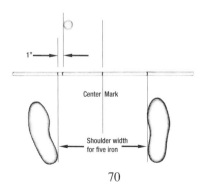

Fig. 35.

Your first drill is not difficult, but it must be learned and monitored. You will need a wooden dowel one-half inch or five-eighths of an inch in diameter and 36 inches long or a 48-inch fiberglass driveway reflector stick (available at most hardware stores) and a felt-tip pen.

Measure your shoulder width by measuring the distance from the outside of your left shoulder to the outside of your right shoulder. It will be roughly 14–20 inches. Using the felt-tip pen, make a center mark on the dowel. Now, make a mark for each shoulder, centered on the dowel (e.g., if your shoulder dimension is 18 inches, one mark should be nine inches left of the center mark, and the other nine inches right of the center mark). This is the distance your heels should be apart at address when setting up with a five-iron. This will give you a constant foot-to-shoulder relationship.

Next, make a third mark one-half to one inch to the right or backward from the left heel mark. This will be your constant ball position no matter where your right foot is placed.

Set up with the dowel in front of your feet and behind the ball. The dowel also represents the ball/target line, so set it up parallel to your target line, but not aimed AT your target. You want your feet and body set up parallel left of your target with the clubface pointed directly at the target. Make certain your left foot is flared out one-quarter turn and your right foot is perpendicular to the target line. Your nose, sternum, belly button, and zipper will always be centered between your feet, no matter where your right foot is located. (The only time they will be centered on the dowel will be in the five-iron position). This address position is vital to implementing Hogan's *missing piece* with the same feeling every time. Any changes at address will lead to inconsistencies in feel.

Keep this dowel handy and always practice with it. This will help you keep your setup and stance constant and consistent with the foot positions described in *Five Lessons*. The dowel will also help you develop consistent alignment in relation to your target, which is a crucial fundamental. (Note: As we age, we lose flexibility. To help you make a good shoulder and hip turn, it is acceptable to drop your right foot out or farther away from the dowel and also flare it backward or away from the target. Don't worry about this; Hogan also made these changes as he got older, and Clem Darracott's DVD is evidence of this.)

The *missing piece* setup leads us into the *final missing piece* of his secret puzzle. Hogan moved forward before he got to the top of his swing. This is easy to see from a good rearview sequence of his swing, and it's vital to understanding his motion.

Because Hogan completed his move before he got to the top of the backswing, he could simply turn his hips to start his downswing, as he said more than 40 times in *Five Lessons*. If a player does not move forward as he turns and continues to the top, he will be forced to make two motions in the downswing: slide and then rotate. Hogan made his forward move with such grace that you might not have noticed until you knew what to look for. Now it's time for you to learn it.

Drill 2 – Proper Hip Turn

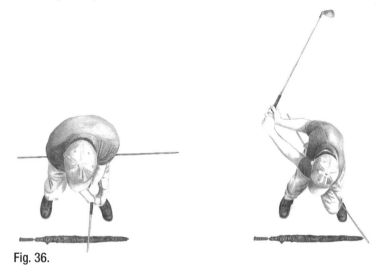

Fig. 36.

This drill is a must. Using your center of gravity effectively in the *missing piece* is dependent on hip turn. You can use this drill to help you better understand hip rotation, and it should be done regularly as long as you play golf. It's a key fundamental. Turn your hips 45 degrees clockwise on your backswing and then start your downswing by turning them counterclockwise.

Use the wooden dowel or fiberglass driveway reflector stick from drill 1 and an 18-inch bungee cord. Hold the dowel across your front hip bones and attach the bungee cord to one side of the dowel. Wrap the bungee cord around your back and attach the other hook to the dowel. The dowel will be parallel to your hips, and you will be able to see how much your hips are turning.

With or without a club, turn to the top of your swing. Note where the stick is pointing. On full swings, the hips should turn 45 degrees from their original starting position. I suggest that you spend five minutes doing this drill every day, making certain that you turn your hips 45 degrees. You'll need to spend a total of five hours doing this drill until you start to master it, and then you'll have to keep performing it to maintain the proper motion. Don't rely on feel when you can be precise. Note: Your spine should NOT be vertical, but tilted back away from the target at the top of the swing (figure 38). If the head does not move forward during the backswing, the spine will tilt backward more than the original angle set at address. This is correct.

Drill 3 – Proper Sequence

The sequencing of the pivot comes next. You can use the stick and bungee cord from drill 2, but it is not mandatory. You will rehearse this "dance step"— as I like to call it— thousands of times. If you aren't careful, you may even do it in public without realizing it. Chances are someone will notice you practicing this move and wonder what the heck are you doing. The sequence of the *missing piece* is very important for the choreography of this dance step to be correct. It's also a different step than you've likely been taught before. Most of us have been instructed to move backward and turn on the backswing, and then to move forward and turn on the downswing.

When using the *missing piece*, you move forward and turn on the backswing, and then simply turn your hips on the downswing. There are many things going on inside the body that you and I cannot see, so you'll need to pay close attention to create the same sequencing as Hogan. The first move is a slight movement of the right hip, a bump if you will, laterally backward. When the hands reach a point waist high, your hips should begin to turn AS THEY MOVE LATERALLY FORWARD. Note the emphasis: TURN AS YOU

MOVE FORWARD. Once at the top of the backswing, we know very well what Hogan would say: JUST TURN YOUR HIPS TO START THE DOWNSWING. Note: at the end of the backswing, it is important to complete your hip turn and arm swing AT THE SAME TIME.

Here's an important detail: Most golfers have a tendency to rush into moving forward and turning. Take your time so that you master the sequence. The forward move-and-turn does not begin until the club is parallel to the ground on the backswing.

Let's practice this: Move into your address position. Start your swing by bumping the right hip one inch or so to the right as your hands move the club away from the ball. NOW, PAUSE! Do this over and over again! I often see people moving too fast to learn this, so take your time.

When you have practiced and perfected the BUMP, continue to move the club until it is parallel to the ground, and THEN BEGIN TO TURN AS YOU MOVE LEFT until your center of gravity is over the inside of your left foot. Again I caution you against going too fast. Take your time.

Do this drill over and over again in front of a mirror so that you can see what you look like. Bump backward one inch during the first 12 inches your hands move in the backswing. When your hands reach waist high, turn and move forward simultaneously until your center of gravity is over the inside of your left foot. It is best to use the bungee cord and the stick. Getting the sequence correct is as important as any other part of the *missing piece*. It should be practiced with great care. You'll need to spend 10 hours doing this drill correctly before you can even THINK that you OWN what Hogan created.

A note here on the sequence: I believe that one of the reasons that Hogan's *missing piece* remained a mystery was that he moved with such beautiful rhythm. If you want to look like Hogan, perform drills 2 and 3 until you feel like you yourself could have taught him how to do them.

Drill 4 – Learn and Practice the Missing Piece

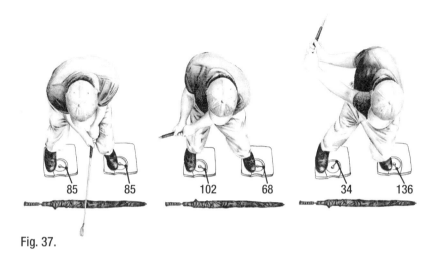

Fig. 37.

Get two inexpensive scales. (They should cost less than $20 each at a discount store.) Space the scales apart and take a stance on the scales just as you would when setting up to the ball. The inside of your heels should be spaced apart the width of your shoulders. Standing on the scales at address, your weight should be evenly distributed between the scales. During the start-up of your swing, shift about 10 percent more of your total weight onto your right foot. It will show up on the scale, but only briefly. Your right hip will move slightly backward.

Once your hands are waist high, start to turn your hips as you move forward. This is important, for the correct sequence of motion can be tough to accomplish if done too fast.

NOTICE THAT YOU TURN AS YOU MOVE FORWARD. YOU DO NOT MOVE FORWARD AND THEN TURN, OR TURN AND THEN MOVE FORWARD.

The turning of the hips and the forward motion are one and the same; they should be done simultaneously. By the time you get to the top, you should have about 80 percent of your weight on the forward scale (your left foot) and about 20 percent on the back scale (inside edge of your right foot).

The sequence of these first two steps is vital: move your weight slightly onto the right foot in the first 12 inches of your backswing.

When your hands are waist high, start to turn your hips AS you move forward to the top of the swing. Do this over and over. This is the most important motion in your new golf swing, and it will feel different from any swing motion that you have ever performed.

It's very common for students of the *missing piece* to ask: "Where am I moving TO?" This simple motion allows you to move most of your weight onto your left foot. With Hogan's constant ball location, your left shoulder will always be in front of the golf ball, and you can then start your downswing like Hogan did, by turning your hips.

If your center of gravity has not moved forward on the backswing, then you must slide forward before turning your hips in the downswing, or you will run into problems and your hands must compensate for this pivot error. Touring pros can perform this slide repeatedly a high percentage of the time, but even they have difficulty with this pivotal moment of the swing when they occasionally lean too far into their right leg at the top, and then suffer from the dreaded pull-hook.

Drill 5 – The Chair Drill—More Pivot Practice

Fig. 38.

As we have seen, Hogan moved his body very efficiently. He turned his hips and moved them forward with determination and confidence, which you should try to copy when moving your own lower body. To create this unified forward and turning movement of the hips and center of gravity, you must master the sequence, feel, and timing of the *final missing piece*. The chair drill makes it possible to practice it anywhere, anytime.

Any kind of chair will do. Place the back of the chair an inch or so from your right hip. This will enable you to move slightly backward during the start of the swing. Now get into your address posture by bending from the hips and imagining that you have a golf club in your hands.

I caution you against doing this exercise too quickly and without checking yourself in a mirror. I have seen golfers who BELIEVED they were practicing the correct thing, but they were in fact only looking funny in front of their fellow employees at work. Follow these simple rules and you will maximize your learning capacity.

1. Set up the chair one inch from your right hip.
2. Get into a good golf posture.
3. Move your hands one foot in the backswing.
4. Your right hip should now be against the chair.

STOP. Feel where you are in space; let your body get accustomed to this movement by holding it for a brief second.

For the next movement to the top, connect your hands and hips together in your mind and physically as shown in figure 38. When your hands are waist high on their path to the top, your hips MUST TURN as they MOVE FORWARD. Your head will lower, but do not let it move forward. Check this constantly in a mirror.

Hogan began his forward motion when the shaft of the club was essentially hip high; this timing of the hands and body cannot be overlooked and must be practiced diligently. STOP when you get to the top, and look down. The hips should be well away from the chair, at least six to ten inches. When I practice this drill, I try to get my hips as far away from the chair as I can, and turn them 45 degrees. Also, as you learned in drill 3, the hip turn and forward motion must finish at the same time, at the end of the backswing.

The reason for a six to ten inches range is that the actual hip movement depends on the width of your stance. This drill coordinates your hands with your body. You are learning the rhythm, pace, and timing required to move your upper and lower body in unison. You are learning the "dance step" of the body motion while getting 80 percent of your weight forward and over your left leg. You are getting accustomed to the feel so that on the golf course you can just let it go and never hit the ball left again.

I would recommend that you do this drill forever. Use it to monitor your body and as insurance against your old motion. Use it to build the proper rhythm and timing for the coordinated movement of the hands and body. Use it more than your television remote, and you WILL hit better golf shots.

Drill 6 – Making Sure Your Arms and Hands Work Correctly

Fig. 39.

The "driver-off-the-knees" drill is associated with trick-shot artists, but it is one of the best for showing you how to use your hands and arms correctly, which is a must for taking full advantage of the *missing piece.*

This drill was demonstrated by Bobby Clampett on the first tee at the 1979 U.S. Open (much to the chagrin of the USGA), by Seve Ballesteros in the 1990 *PGA Teaching Manual,* and as recently as 2006 when one of Jim Flick's world-class junior golfers performed it on *Academy Live* on the Golf Channel.

One of the best features of this drill is that you can do it at home. All you need is a fairly good net, a piece of carpet to kneel on and hit from, some rubber driving range tees, and a 10x15-foot space in your garage, basement, or game room.

With this drill, you can hit a lot of balls with a full swing and avoid the impact stress on your hands and wrists that occurs when you hit irons from a driving range mat.

The drill is simple. Make a smooth swing on an almost horizontal plane and let your hands work as shown on pages 98, 99, and 102 of *Five Lessons.* To do the drill, get on your knees, place the ball on the rubber tee in the center of your body, and swing. If you swing incorrectly, you will have difficulty making a full and smooth swing because your hands and arms will restrict a fluid motion. Swing correctly, and the motion will feel natural and easy.

This drill is also an excellent way to keep your muscles and your swing in shape when you cannot get to a range or golf course regularly.

Conclusion

Changing your golf swing is more difficult than most amateurs realize, but it is possible if you put in the time and effort. The above drills are effective because they isolate specific motions that you are trying to learn and you are not distracted by ball flight. They also don't take a significant amount of time, but when done consistently over a sustained period they will help you learn your new swing. Finally, they can all be done at home—you don't have to go to a golf course every day to improve. As inspiration, think of how Hogan dug his swing out of the dirt by practicing relentlessly. If you have big golf dreams, you have to put in big-time effort. The payoff is certainly worth it.

Chapter 11

Does Hogan's Swing Still Apply to the Modern Golfer?

The answer is definitely "yes." The laws of physics have not changed in the 320 years since Newton discovered them, and they certainly haven't changed since the 1950s. The physics that gave Hogan his tremendous power and amazing control work today just as well as they did then.

For further proof, you can compare post-accident rearview swing sequences of Hogan and a recent multiple winner on the PGA Tour from the waist down, side by side. You will note a very similar leg action, even though one of these golfers is swinging on legs that were almost destroyed in a car wreck, while the other is a world-class athlete in the prime of his career.

A noted television announcer and swing analyst recently described this same player as having the best body rotation through the ball of any player on the PGA Tour. This is another confirmation that the swing of Ben Hogan is still relevant today.

In this era of high-speed video cameras, 460 cc composite drivers, long golf balls that barely curve, and thousands of competent golf instructors, there is still a place for Hogan's golf swing. The golf public agrees; yearly sales of *Five Lessons* are still brisk.

Now, with the discoveries that we've made, it's our humble opinion that *Five Lessons* is even more valuable and helpful to the hundreds of thousands of golfers who own a copy.

However, with all due respect, you'll have to delete or ignore some information from *Five Lessons* that has been shown to be misleading or inaccurate.

1. On page 75 of *Five Lessons*, cross out the two images of Hogan practicing his backswing without moving his right hip back laterally. When he returned to competition after his car wreck, Hogan did NOT do what is illustrated on page 75. Replace these images with the umbrella-hip images in figure 40.

Fig. 40 - What Ben Hogan actually did

2. Ignore the three times Hogan says to move your weight from your right to your left foot (pages 90 and 92 of *Five Lessons*). Instead, move most of your weight onto your left foot during your backswing as Hogan actually did in figure 41, then start your downswing by turning your hips, as he instructed more than 40 times in the book.

BUMP   TURN AND MOVE   ROTATE

Fig. 41.

3. Ignore the IMAGE of the shifted downswing plane on page 88 of *Five Lessons*, but embrace the FEELING of it. Use this feeling to swing beneath the shallower downswing plane, then strike the inside of the ball, like Hogan actually did, then make sure your arms go left and do not separate from the body as shown in figure 42.

Fig. 42 - Note: Ben Hogan's arms do not swing to the right after impact.

With these minor modifications, *Five Lessons* can become the ultimate golf swing instruction book that it was always destined to be.

Stack and Tilt? - Definitely Not!

Finally, while discussing the modern-day golfer, it is important to understand that Hogan's *missing piece* is very different from the latest swing technique on the PGA Tour, the "stack and tilt." Both of these swings incorporate a minimal backward weight shift on the backswing, but from here any similarities cease. The stack and tilt requires a forward tilted spine at the top of the swing, while the *missing piece* swing requires a spine which is angled backward, AWAY from the target at the top. Also, Hogan moved his weight forward during the BACKSWING, so that he could start his downswing by simply turning his hips. The stack and tilt (as with almost all other modern instruction) utilizes a forward weight shift on the DOWNSWING, either prior to or during the counterclockwise turning of the hips.

Chapter 12

Why Did It Take 57 Years to Discover the Missing Piece?

There are four main reasons why it took 57 years to discover the *missing piece*.

1. Everyone was looking in the wrong place. A good example of this can be seen in the image of Ben Hogan in figure 3 on page 13. Front-on camera angles provide a very poor perspective from which to study his golf swing. The increased angle of his right leg is not immediately obvious, nor is his weight shift over to his left leg, unless you know what to look for.

Also, when Hogan's swing is viewed in videos and photographs from face-on (as if we were standing in front of him), his body appears to move forward at the start of his downswing. What we are actually seeing is his rapid hip rotation and his left hip returning to its wider, full frontal width. This makes it appear that he moves forward to start his downswing when actually his weight was already fully forward and he was simply turning his hips to start his downswing, as he says to do in *Five Lessons*.

This can be proven by looking at rearview sequences of Hogan's swing in figure 43. From this vantage point, the white spot above his right hip pocket actually moves backward or away from the target at the start of his downswing. If his hips had moved forward to start the downswing, this white spot would also move forward or at least stay in the same position.

Fig. 43 - Note: Ben Hogan started his downswing with a pure rotation of his hips.

The Math of the Hip Turn

If Hogan had slid forward to start his downswing and THEN turned, the white spot above his right rear pocket would have moved forward approximately four and one-half inches due to this hip slide and backward one and one-half inches (FHM - (1/2 HCL-HL2) = 4 1/2″ - (5″ - 3 1/2″) = 3″, see pages 87 and 88) due to his hips returning to their initial position. This would be a net FORWARD movement of three inches.

You can see from figure 43 that this DID NOT happen. The white spot actually MOVED BACKWARD as the downswing began.

2. There were few high-quality videos of his swing, and he was very careful whom he allowed to film his swing. Hogan is said to have turned down CBS Television's request to film his swing during his last Masters appearance in 1967, yet he allowed Clem Darracott to film it on a home movie camera. Also, there were no reliable weight-shift recorders available at the time. With the electronic measuring devices and super-high-speed cameras available today, his *final missing piece* would have been impossible to keep secret.

3. As we have mentioned, some instructors and professionals have described Hogan's swing as having a reverse pivot. Nothing could be further from the truth. Hogan's weight DEFINITELY did not move backward during his downswing, as would have occurred if he had a reverse pivot. Such comments have discouraged many from trying to duplicate his swing or studying it further to discover what he actually was doing.

4. Finally, his hip action was so fast that we could not see what he was doing with the naked eye. Many of his contemporaries commented on his hip speed during his swing; this is clearly evident when you watch a full-speed video of Hogan hitting a golf ball. If you do not know exactly where to look, his secret is buried in a blur.

All of these contributed to one of the greatest mysteries in golf— one that lasted 57 years. And by the way, now that you know where to look, it is easy to see.

Chapter 13

Did Hogan Realize His Book Did Not Show What He Actually Did?

Was Hogan aware that his book did not show what he actually did? What do you think?

During his era of dominance, many people in the golf world felt that Hogan knew more about the golf swing than anyone else in the world and that *Five Lessons* confirmed his status when his competitive days were over. It is hard to imagine that such a person would not know that some of the drawings in *Five Lessons* did not reflect his actual swing.

He posed for photographs for artist Anthony Ravielli to work from. He had to know exactly how Ravielli's realist style would record his swing for the book. These images left out the *missing piece* of his secret.

You'll recall that a number of Hogan's contemporaries believed that he intentionally played coy in his discussions of the "secret" during his playing days and that they didn't believe that his 1955 *Life* article fully disclosed it.

We have noted that Hogan mentions starting the downswing by turning the hips—or similar references connecting the hips to the downswing—more than 40 times in *Five Lessons*. However, on only three occasions does he talk about a forward weight shift and a hip turn in the same paragraph. On page 90, he states in capital letters that the weight must move laterally or forward. A careful reading of this paragraph reveals that Hogan does not say exactly WHEN this must happen, only that it HAS to happen.

It is our belief that he was so protective of the *final missing piece* that he consciously withheld sharing it. However, Hogan likely knew that if he did NOT mention weight shift, he would be raising a red flag among golf professionals and readers who had expert knowledge of the golf swing.

Hogan knew he had to mention something about weight transfer, and by stating something so boldly on page 90 in capital letters, it appears that he attempted to eliminate efforts to connect his pivot and the timing of his weight transfer to his "secret."

Yet, on almost 40 other occasions he said to start your swing with a turning of the hips, with no specific reference to a forward weight shift. This ratio (39 to 3) should be a good indication of his true beliefs regarding the importance of starting his downswing by TURNING HIS HIPS, and not with a lateral, forward movement of his weight.

We believe that Hogan sincerely believed that he was providing so much new, precise, and exciting information about the golf swing that even without his "secret," the book could benefit millions of golfers. We will never know for sure, but he may also have believed that anyone who wanted to discover what we've called the *final missing piece* would have to "dig it out of the dirt," just like he did.

It is hard to fault him for that.

Appendix

The Math Behind the Shallower Downswing Plane and the Lowered, Sitting-Down Look

Below is the math which explains why Ben Hogan's head and body measurement is lower at the top of his swing than at set-up, as evidenced in three different pictures in this book (figures 13, 24, and 25). His heel-to-heel spacing (HHS1) was scaled from pictures 1 and 8, figure 15, using his biographical height of five feet seven inches.

The resulting heel-to-heel spacing of 19.61″ was then used to create a new scale for figures 23 and 24 of 1″ = 29.94″, and this scale was used for the lower body math.

The upper body calculations are based on figure 25 and are scaled using Ben Hogan's known driver length of 42.875″[xxii]. This gives us a scale of 1″ = 22.685″ (42.875″ / 1.890″ = 22.685″), and the upper body math is based on this scale.

Basic Measurements: (pictures 1 and 8, figure 15, pages 40-41)
Body height = 2.460″ = 67″ : Scale: 1″ = 27.236″
Heel-to-heel spacing = HHS1 = .720″ = 19.61″

Lower Body Math: (triangles from page 55)

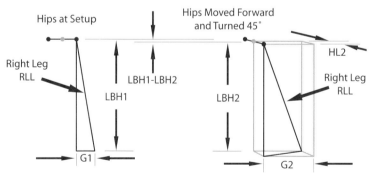

Fig. 44 - Lower body math (not to scale)

Lower body rescaled measurements: (figures 23 and 24, page 55)
Heel to heel spacing = HHS2 = .655″ = 19.61″
New scale 1″ = 29.94″

(Continued on next page)

Lower Body Math: (continued)

Hip joint centerline (est.) = HCL = 10″ = .334″
Forward hip movement = FHM = X-Y = (.290″-.144″) x 29.94″ = 4.37″
Scaled lowering (figure 24) = .065″ x 29.94″ = 1.95″

G1 = 1/2HHS2 - 1/2HCL = 1/2 x 19.61 - 1/2 x 10 = 4.81″
G2 = 1/2 HHS2 + FHM - 1/2HCL / 2 = 1/2 x 19.61 + 4.37 - 5 / 1.41 = 10.64″
HL2 = 1/2HCL / 2 = 5 / 1.414 = 3.54″

$RLL^2 = G1^2 + LBH1^2$	$RLL^2 = G2^2 + LBH2^2 + HL2^2$
$LBH1 = \sqrt{RLL^2 - G1^2}$	$LBH2 = \sqrt{RLL^2 - G2^2 - HL2^2}$
$LBH1 = \sqrt{37.19^2 - 4.81^2}$	$LBH2 = \sqrt{37.19^2 - 10.64^2 - 3.54^2}$
$LBH1 = 36.88″$	$LBH2 = 35.46″$

Calculated (LBH1 - LBH2) = 36.88″ - 35.46″ = 1.42″

Upper Body Math: (triangles from page 56)

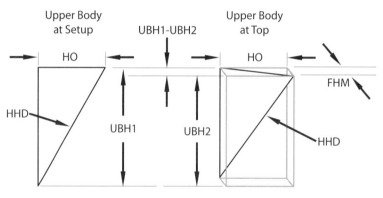

Fig. 45 - Upper body math (not to scale)

Upper body scaled measurements: (figure 25, page 56)
Driver length[xxii] = DL = 42.875″ = 1.890″
Scale: 1″ = 22.685″
Head offset = HO = .720″ = 16.33″
Upper body height at setup = UBH1 = 1.254″ = 28.45″
Hip-head distance = HHD = 1.438″ = 32.62″
Forward hip movement = FHM = 4.37″ (same as for lower body)
Scaled lowering (figure 25) = .092″ x 22.685″ = 2.09″

$HHD^2 = HO^2 + UBH2^2 + FHM^2$
$UBH2 = \sqrt{HHD^2 - HO^2 - FHM^2}$
$UBH2 = \sqrt{32.62^2 - 16.33^2 - 4.37^2}$
$UBH2 = 27.90″$

Total lowering, head and body:
= (LBH1 - LBH2) + (UBH1 - UBH2)
= (36.88″ - 35.40″) + (28.45″ - 27.90″)
= 1.42″ + .55″ = 1.97″

Calculated (UBH1 - UBH2) = 28.45″ - 27.90″ = .55″
Calculated total lowering = 1.42″ + .55″ = 1.97″

Notes

i   Dodson, James, *Ben Hogan: An American Life*, p 126.

ii   Hogan, Ben, "This Is My Secret," *Life*, 1955, p 61.

iii   Stolley, Dick, "Ben Hogan's Secret," *Life*, 1954, p131.

iv   Stolley, Dick, "Ben Hogan's Secret," *Life*, 1954, p 134.

v   Wind, Herbert Warren, *The Story of American Golf*, p 354.

vi   Wind, Herbert Warren, *The Story of American Golf*, p 354.

vii   Middlecoff, Cary, *The Golf Swing*, p 80.

viii   Middlecoff, Cary, *The Golf Swing*, p 80.

ix   Stolley, Dick, "Ben Hogan's Secret," *Life*, 1954, p 126.

x   Stolley, Dick, "Ben Hogan's Secret," *Life*, 1954, p129.

xi   Stolley, Dick, "Ben Hogan's Secret," *Life*, 1954, p 132.

xii   Hogan, Ben, "This Is My Secret," *Life*, 1955, p 61.

xiii   Hogan, Ben, "This Is My Secret," *Life*, 1955, p 62.

xiv   Wind, Herbert Warren, *The Story of American Golf*, p 368.

xv   Hogan, Ben, "This Is My Secret," *Life*, 1955, p 62.

xvi   *American Heritage Dictionary*, 1985, p 253.

xvii   Fields, Bill, "A Champion's Last Hurrah," *Golf World*, 2007, p 57.

xviii   Fields, Bill, "A Champion's Last Hurrah," *Golf World*, 2007, p 54.

xix   Hogan, Ben, *Five Lessons*, p 93.

xx   Hogan, Ben, *Five Lessons*, p 93.

xxi   Hogan, Ben, *Five Lessons*, p 91.

xxii   Sampson, Curt, *Hogan*, p 208.

Bibliography

American Heritage Dictionary. Boston, Mass.: Houghton Mifflin Co., 1985.

Andrisani, John. *The Hogan Way*. New York: HarperCollins, 2000.

Bertrand, Tom. *The Secret of Hogan's Swing*. Hoboken, N.J.: John Wiley & Sons, 2006.

Darracott, Clem. *Ben Hogan: In Pursuit of Perfection*. DVD. Clem Darracott Incorporated, 1995.

Davis, Martin. *Ben Hogan: The Man behind the Mystique*. Greenwich, Conn.: The American Golfer, Inc., 2002.

Davis, Martin. *The Hogan Mystique*. Triumph Books, 1994.

Dodson, James. *Ben Hogan: An American Life*. New York: Doubleday, 2004.

Fields, Bill. "A Champions Last Hurrah". *Golf World*, March 30, 2007, 52—57

Gregston, Gene. *Hogan: The Man Who Played for Glory*. Englewood Cliffs, N.J.: Prentice Hall, 1978.

Hebron, Michael. *See and Feel the Inside Move the Outside*. Smithtown, N.Y.: Rost Associates, 1984.

Hogan, Ben. *Five Lessons: The Modern Fundamentals of Golf*. New York: Cornerstone Library, 1957.

Hogan, Ben. *Power Golf*. Cranbury, N.J.: A. S. Barnes & Co., 1948.

Hogan, Ben. "This Is My Secret." *Life*, August 8, 1955, 61–63.

Jones, Ernest. *Swing the Clubhead*. New York: Dodd, Mead & Co., 1952

Kelley, Homer. *The Golfing Machine*. Beverton, Ore.: Star System Press, 1969.

Leadbetter, David. *The Fundamentals of Hogan*. Chelsea, Mich.: Sleeping Bear Press; New York: Doubleday, 2000.

McCarthy, Tom. *The Ben Hogan Collection*. Miami, Fl.: McTee's Champions, LLC, 206.

Mehlhorn, Bill. *Golf Secrets Exposed*. Miami, Fl.: M & S Publishing, 1984.

Middlecoff, Cary. *The Golf Swing*. New York: Simon and Schuster, 1974.

Newton, Sir Isaac. *Mathematical Principles of Natural Philosophy*. 1687.

Nicklaus, Jack. *Golf My Way*. New York: Simon and Schuster, 1974.

Ogata, Katsuhiko. *System Dynamics*. Englewood Cliffs, N.J.: Prentice-Hall, 1978.

Sampson, Curt. *Hogan*. Nashville, Tenn.: Rutledge Hill Press, 1996.

Shoemaker, Fred. *Extraordinary Golf: The Art of the Possible*. New York: G. P. Putnam's Sons, 1996.

Snead, Sam. *How to Play Golf*. New York: Garden City Publishing, 1946.

Stolley, Dick. "Ben Hogan's Secret." *Life*, August 8, 1955, 126–134.

Towle, Mike. *I Remember Ben Hogan*. Nashville, Tenn.: Cumberland House, 2000.

Wind, Herbert Warren. *The Story of American Golf: Its Champions and Championships*. 3rd ed. New York: Knopf, 1975.

Wiren, Gary. *PGA Teaching Manual*: Palm Beach Gardens, Fla.: PGA of America, 1990.

About the Authors

V.J. Trolio is a Class A member of the PGA and the teaching professional at Old Waverly Golf Club in West Point, Mississippi. Old Waverly is a *Golf Digest* Top 100 Golf Club and host of the 1999 USGA Women's Open and the 2006 USGA Women's Mid-Amateur.

V.J. lives in West Point with his wife Allison and their two sons.

He played college golf at the University of Southern Mississippi, where he set the career scoring average of 72.79 and qualified for the NCAA Regionals his senior year.

As a pro he has won the Gulf States Assistants Championship three times and finished second in the National Assistants Championship in 2004 and third in 2002. Since adding the missing piece to his own golf swing, he has won the 2007 Mississippi Open (Farm Bureau Invitational).

He works with golfers of all ability levels, from young beginners to touring pros on the PGA Tour.

V.J. is co-inventor of the Putting Arc®. He can be contacted at troliogolf.com

Dave Hamilton holds a degree in electrical engineering from Cornell University, where he was captain of the golf team. He lives in Mississippi with his wife Maggie. They have two children and eight grandchildren. He has seven golf-related patents, including the Putting Arc® and the putting robot, Iron Archie™.

This book was edited by Tim O'Connor. He lives in Rockwood, Ontario, Canada, with his wife Sandy and their two sons. Tim is the author of *The Feeling of Greatness: The Moe Norman Story.*

About This Book

Ben Hogan had many secrets, and he used them to create a puzzle, which he gave to the golf world in the form of his book, *Five Lessons: The Modern Fundamentals of Golf.* According to most accounts, this great book has become the top-selling instructional book of all time in any sport.

In this book he revealed the secrets which took him to the pinnacle of golfing excellence. However, somehow he left out one final piece of this puzzle, the *final missing piece* that makes everything else work. He left it up to the rest of the world to dig it out of the dirt, just like he had to do, and for the past 57 years this *missing piece* has remained cleverly hidden.

Ben Hogan was quoted in *Life* magazine in 1954: "I have a secret" and "It is easy to see, if I tell you where to look." With this book you can look in the correct place, for the correct things, and understand the genius behind this secret.

Now you can finally fill in the *missing piece* of Ben Hogan's secret puzzle and apply this amazing secret to your own golf game. If you have been studying *Five*

Lessons and are already able to do what the book teaches, then this *final missing piece* will very quickly take your swing and your whole attitude about golf to an exciting new level.

•Learn how Ben Hogan applied Newton's Second Law of Physics to create his tremendous power.

•Learn which critical fundamentals you should embrace from *Five Lessons* and which pages you should ignore in order to swing a golf club like Ben Hogan.

•Learn Ben Hogan's one secret move that eliminated the unintended hook and took the left side of the course out of play.

•Learn how to automatically create Ben Hogan's downswing plane, which ensures an inside attack on the golf ball.

•Learn the math and science behind Ben Hogan's lowered, sitting-down look and the shallower downswing plane he refers to in *Five Lessons*.

Testimonials from golfers who have experienced the *final missing piece*.

"When I was playing my best golf, I was told that I had Hogan-like mechanics, but not until I started working with V. J. Trolio did I truly understand what Hogan-like mechanics are. Thanks to V.J. my golf swing has returned to its original form."
Jim Gallagher, Jr. - Five-time PGA Tour Champion

"What a great book! Through great dedication and determination you have risen to the top of the field. You have overcome many things in life and I am very proud of all your accomplishments. I wish you great success with this book. Congratulations!"
Randy Watkins - PGA National Junior Champion (1977),
PGA TOUR 1984-1985, Class A PGA Professional,
Tournament Director - PGA TOUR's Viking Classic

"Over the years I have tried many things to create a better golf swing. In this book, Hogan's radically different swing sequence is revealed, and it was this *missing piece* that made golf fun for me again."
Chris Jester - Class A PGA Professional

**Available at: www.TheFinalMissingPiece.com
Distributed by: The Putting Arc, Inc.
www.ThePuttingArc.com
800-898-0701 M-F 9-5 EST**